May 2011

"FEED THE FUTURE": RESEARCH STRATEGY

TABLE OF CONTENTS

Executive Summary

The President's Global Hunger and Food Security Initiative, titled "Feed the Future (FTF)", has the overarching goal of sustainably reducing global poverty and hunger (www.feedthefuture.gov). Providing sufficient food to the world's growing population will require a 70 percent increase in agricultural production by 2050 (Bruinsma 2009). To meet this food security challenge under constraints of limited agricultural land availability and increased climatic variability, the world will need to support and develop scientific and technological innovations that increase agricultural productivity in an environmentally sound manner while improving the availability of nutritious foods. The food price spikes of 2006-2008 and that are resurfacing today underscore the fragility of global food security, with recent estimates that nearly a billion people are food insecure (Shapouri 2010), affecting families in the United States and around the world. While the causes were many, the underlying challenges are clear: the world cannot achieve the Millennium Development Goals (http://www.un.org/millenniumgoals/) relating to hunger, poverty, health, gender and the environment when the growth of agricultural productivity and income stagnates or is otherwise insufficient.

The global research portfolio, presented here, serves as an integral strategy within the broader *Feed the Future* Initiative. The FTF Initiative includes targeted investments in Focus Countries to enhance agricultural productivity, to expand markets and trade, and to increase the economic resilience of vulnerable rural communities in addition to supporting a multifaceted approach to nutrition. The FTF Initiative will make complementary investments in regional programs where food security issues go beyond national boundaries, multilateral mechanisms for large-scale investments such as infrastructure, and strategic partnerships with countries that serve as regional anchors for food security.

Research investments described in this strategy will focus on international public goods, which will benefit Focus Country producers and consumers as well as those in neighboring countries. International public goods research will be linked to investments in Focus Countries in local adaptive research, institutional and human capacity building and strengthening of extension services. These country-level investments are central to the successful utilization of the outputs of research. Operational dimensions and linkages between the global research portfolio and national level programs will need to be worked out in each country in ways that fully reflect the country-led approach.

A. Why research?

Research figures prominently in the *Feed the Future Initiative* because it is critical to sustainably enhancing agricultural productivity growth, which is strongly linked to economic growth in developing countries and has shown substantial impact on reducing poverty in Asia and Africa (Thirtle et al. 2003). Ensuring global food security will only become more difficult given the challenges associated with providing sufficient food for a growing global population. In addition, growth in agricultural productivity faces increasing challenges from land degradation, climate change, scarce water supplies, and competition for energy resources from industry and urbanization. In addition to the linkages among agricultural productivity, agriculture-led economic development and poverty reduction, we also recognize the multiple interacting direct and indirect pathways through which agricultural research can contribute to improved nutrition. Solutions lie in research to achieve sustainable intensification through increases in agricultural productivity with an emphasis on improving the nutritional quality of the diet while reducing agriculture's adverse impact on natural resources and the environment. Environmentally and economically sustainable agricultural productivity gains will be generated from a range of innovations, including resource use efficiency, genetic improvement, integrated pest management, reduced post-harvest losses, risk management strategies, and reduced marketing costs. These innovations will be developed and deployed in close collaboration with stakeholders from national governments to local communities to ensure that technologies and innovations developed are responsive to the needs of poor producers in our partner countries.

Impact: Investing in agricultural research today will contribute to the growth and resilience of the food supply tomorrow. When combined with effective extension services and appropriate market incentives, agricultural research increases agricultural productivity (affecting the availability of food) but also increases real income to purchase food (impacting household access to food) and, potentially, the quality of the diet consumed (associated with human nutritional status). Moreover, increased agricultural productivity drives demand for goods and services, especially those produced locally, helping generate employment and further reducing poverty. Agricultural research and technology deployment accompanied by investments in extension, education and other activities that spur rural enterprises are very effective in driving broad-based economic growth, which can especially benefit low-income groups.

Scale: Since outputs from global research have broad applicability, they can be adapted over wide areas to increase agricultural productivity. Collectively, agriculture productivity and efficiency gains can add tens of billions of dollars to developing countries' economies and food security annually. Direct and indirect income gains, multiplied year after year, lead to rural transformation through increased demands for locally produced goods and services. Past research indicates high rates of return from agricultural research in Sub-Saharan Africa, averaging between 22-34 percent per year (Alston et al. 2000, Thirtle et al. 2003).
The growth in agricultural GDP generated by productivity gains provides broad impact across the economy, for both producers and consumers.

B. What is new?

The global research strategy under the *Feed the Future* Initiative is one part of the larger *Feed the Future* strategy and will be implemented in close coordination with other programs in the Initiative. *Feed the Future's* research portfolio emphasizes a new paradigm of sustainable intensification to catalyze agriculture-led economic growth by focusing on environmentally-sustainable productivity gains through research that is purpose-driven and impact-oriented, and that operates in close coordination with deployment of research outputs through extension, education, evaluation and feedback at the individual country level. Our strategy calls for closer ties and sharing of information across the three stages of research—discovery, development and deployment. This includes the integration of natural science and social science research including policy analysis to increase impacts for developing world farmers.

The approach also emphasizes building linkages and collaborations across the U.S. and international research communities and helping to leverage U.S. public and private research investments with the investments made by others. We will work closely with other research donors such as foundations, the private sector, and governments to target common priorities to enhance agricultural productivity and sustainability.

Whole of Government: *Feed the Future* adopts a new whole of government approach to leverage the existing competencies of USG agencies toward the common goals of reducing poverty and hunger. The Department of State, the U.S. Agency for International Development and the U.S. Department of Agriculture have worked together to develop this strategy. USG agencies will work together to implement the FTF research strategy, including, where appropriate, aligning their food-security related research programs with the FTF research priorities.

Highlighting Gender: Women play a key role in achieving a food-secure world and our research strategy takes into consideration the needs and roles of women as producers, entrepreneurs, scientists, extension agents, and consumers. Integration of gender analysis and ensuring that benefits are equitably distributed from our investments are critical to achieving our goals of sustainably reducing poverty and hunger. Women often play a significant role in production as well as allocating household resources in ways that have significant benefits to children's nutritional status, and understanding perspectives of both men and women in resource allocation will improve programmatic efforts to increase productivity and improve child nutrition at the household level. In addressing gender and the needs of women as agricultural producers, the FTF research strategy takes into account their access to assets, inputs, and technologies which also, conversely, require that the technologies we are developing respond to potentially differing needs and roles of men and women. We will work to expand the involvement and participation of women in decision-making at all levels and in all institutions, including those dedicated to research and extension. We will advance women's leadership in science and technology through proactive recruitment, mentoring, and targeted research support.

C. What will we do?

Purpose-driven Research: Three research themes have been identified to advance food security and development in service of the broader objectives of *Feed the Future*. These three themes join together in the concept of sustainable intensification:

- **Advancing the productivity frontier:** Improving food availability is underscored in this research theme. While better management practices can reduce the prevailing yield gaps in many developing countries, productivity gains necessary to meet future food demand (under limited resources and with potentially adverse impacts from climate change) require developing new seeds and livestock breeds that push the productivity frontier to the next level. A focus of the FTF research strategy will be on breeding and genetics for major crops and livestock, vaccine development for livestock diseases, and better management policies and practices for fish (both capture fisheries and aquaculture) to increase the yield potential and provide solutions for major production constraints. To more effectively integrate the use of these technologies among poor farmers, research under this theme will encompass socio-behavioral and economic factors related to technology adoption including analysis of incentive structures and policies.

- **Transforming Production Systems:** Sustainable intensification places the agricultural research agenda into a broader context, spanning biophysical, policy and social elements of key production systems where the poor and undernourished are concentrated. Combined with research on natural resources at the systems level, this priority area emphasizes the integration of research advances (e.g., those from priority area 1) within production systems where poverty and malnutrition are concentrated. It also focuses on natural and social science research to examine impacts, particularly interaction effects, of component technologies to increase systems-level productivity and sustainability. Research within the systems context will contribute to improved stability of food production, incomes, and farmer resilience. Key opportunities include research on soil fertility, water and nutrient policy and use, aquaculture and fisheries policy and management, producer safety nets, conservation agriculture, input and output markets, and trade. Many of these areas offer significant opportunities for increasing efficiency and reducing risk.

- **Enhanced nutrition and food safety:** This theme emphasizes the importance of ensuring that agricultural systems contribute to nutrition and health goals. This theme will focus on opportunities to improve availability and access to a high quality diet, particularly for women and young children. Through targeted research in the natural and social sciences, we will focus agricultural systems on improving nutrition through diversification of production systems, enhancing dietary diversity and nutrient density of foods and reducing postharvest losses. This theme will also improve utilization of food through attention to food safety challenges with a focus on reducing contaminants in the food supply. Research priorities in this theme are integrally linked to the first two themes thereby leveraging those investments to ensure the dual focus on improving nutrition and reducing poverty.

D. How will we implement the Strategy?

Country-led: Feed the Future represents the United States' approach to solving problems that will require working with others in both funding and implementation, and most importantly our partners at the national level in Focus Countries. As a country-led effort, our research responds to the analyses and decisions that they have made, for example through the CAADP process in Africa. These national level decisions are aggregated to the regional and global levels, where FTF and other key global and regional research resources and programs respond to them. Sustaining appropriate information and research linkages spanning global, regional, national levels is at the core of FTF research collaboration.

Focus: Research and development under *Feed the Future* will target a broad but well-defined set of food production constraints. Research investments will be of sufficient size to ensure that real progress can be made. Matching resources with the problems is part of an in-depth approach that will also rigorously monitor research milestones to ensure accountability thereby strengthening impact. Given the length of time required for research from inception to impact, it is important to consider how Feed the Future research involves an existing pipeline of research programs, some in early stages and others poised to or already delivering impacts. By linking our research efforts already reaching the impact stage to related investment in strengthening national partnerships, extension, policy and markets, we can help generate demand for new technologies and yield development impacts.

Leadership: The United States is well positioned to marshal the world's largest agricultural research and teaching community—public and private—as partners in a global struggle to achieve lasting food security. *Feed the Future* returns a strong agricultural productivity focus to U.S.-funded agricultural research for development because we know that productivity gains can be reinvigorated based on good technology, sound policy and reinvestment in research and development. We will identify and generate synergies between domestic and international research investments, and join with other major development partners and with developing country and regional research and development organizations to foster shared ownership and to ensure that country, regional, and global investments are integrated for maximal impact.

Research partnerships: The *Feed the Future* research strategy is based on research partnerships that leverage the strengths of partners across the US Government, the private sector, U.S. and non-U.S. universities, Consultative Group on International Agricultural Research (CGIAR) centers, national and regional research programs and NGOs. Through the Norman Borlaug Commemorative Research Initiative, USAID and USDA will lead efforts to strengthen international public goods research in ways that generate technologies and knowledge that support agricultural productivity both in the U.S. and developing countries. Other U.S. Government agencies, such as the National Science Foundation and the National Institutes of Health, are also well positioned to contribute to the broader research objectives and goals of FTF.

In supporting partnerships between US and developing world scientists, we will seek to determine where a comparative advantage exists for solving specific problems through utilizing the capabilities of advanced labs and facilities in the United States that are not available in developing countries. Fostering collaboration among researchers in the developed and developing world will also directly and indirectly build capacity among developing country scientists. To enhance these partnerships, USAID and USDA will work together to identify opportunities for designing complementary programs that increase Feed the Future relevance and impacts of USDA-funded research, generating dual purpose outcomes (benefiting U.S. and developing countries).

Capacity Building: More explicit program linkages to national and regional investments by our partners and through U.S. government overseas missions and offices offer critical means to address both human and institutional impediments to agricultural transformation and food security. We will work directly through collaborative research arrangements that engage developing country partners in ways that build capacity of both women and men. New efforts, through country-level investments from the *Feed the Future* Initiative, will be aimed at strengthening institutional and policy environments, higher education, and addressing constraints along the value-chain from production to market to end-use. These capacity building efforts will complement the research strategy described here by ensuring that linkages are made among U.S. research partners, international research centers, national and regional research, extensions, and education partners as well as relevant user communities at the local level (farmer organizations, NGOs, etc.), including strengthened agricultural producer organizations to better represent the interests of men and women producers.

E. Cross-cutting Issues.

Gender: Best practices show that gender should be integrated at all levels of programs, and research under *Feed the Future* is no different. Creating significant new economic opportunities for women is critical for accelerating growth and achieving a food secure world, and research outcomes designed for women's roles and needs will be required to increase the incomes of women producers.

Climate Change: Agriculture is one of the most climate-dependent of human activities, and hence adaptation and resilience to climate need to be integrated across the research portfolio. At the same time, agriculture can be a driver of climate change, environmental degradation and a major source of emissions, especially with respect to land use change and deforestation. Sustainable agriculture practices can mitigate these negative impacts, for example through enhanced soil organic matter and strategic ecological water storage. Research on climate change concerns will also serve the broader integration effort of FTF activities to increase food security with the President's Global Climate Change for Sustainable Development initiative. There is scope, therefore, for addressing both mitigation and adaptation through strategic investments in agricultural research.

Environment: Ecology is at the heart of sustainable intensification. The FTF research portfolio will integrate technologies, policies and management practices that foster natural resource conservation and productive agriculture in the larger landscape. Both direct and indirect environmental benefits will be considered, for example the beneficial effects of sustainable intensification directly in the production environment, but also its relationship to more fragile environments, both upstream and downstream. This holistic approach, including consideration of the entire watershed management, will better integrate research activity at a scale relevant to all stakeholders in diverse sectors including energy, agriculture and business.

F. Accountability.

We will hold ourselves publicly accountable by regularly measuring and reporting the success of our investments. This process will be part of the FTF Results Framework (RF) with the overarching goal of sustainably reducing global hunger and poverty. Enhanced technology development and dissemination, combined with enhanced human and institutional capacity development and improved policy environments, will contribute to improved agricultural productivity for income growth and greater access to diverse and quality foods for improved nutrition. Among other indicators, outcomes will be measured by the number of farmers (by gender and by income levels) adopting newly available technologies. Research milestones regarding technologies, management practices, and policies under research as well as those subsequently under field testing or released for adoption will be closely monitored.

Conclusion

Research will be critical to achieving our goals for food security, whether through biology, better information and understanding of the social and environmental contexts, or improvements in policies governing access to, management and conservation of increasingly scarce natural resources. Research figures prominently in *Feed the Future* because it is critical to enhancing and sustaining agricultural productivity growth, which is strongly linked to economic growth in developing countries and reduced poverty—both essential elements of sustainable food security.

Success will be defined in agricultural systems that most effectively and efficiently harness fundamental biological, physical, and socio-economic processes in ways that meet the needs of the poor and the hungry. At the same time, these transformations must conserve the resource base in both highly productive and less productive areas. The transformations required to achieve these goals will only be possible if the Initiative is underpinned by innovative research and partnerships.

This document outlines the rationale for a research agenda and criteria for judging research needs and opportunities, leading to a sound basis for strategic choices. It provides examples of the resulting priorities in order to illustrate how the strategy can be put into practice. In addition, the document seeks to highlight opportunities for partnership across research providers with different but complementary capabilities. Thus the intention is to encourage strategic alignment of research investments with Feed the Future goals, recognizing that specific situations will require taking a variety of factors into account. With additional information on country priorities, resource levels and existing program objectives, strategic planning within given programming efforts can be undertaken. In addition, although the strategy has been developed to guide U.S. federal research investments associated with Feed the Future, an on-going and robust dialogue with partners across the U.S. and international research communities will both foster broader relevance of the strategy as well as shape the nature of specific investments and partnerships that result from it. Through close coordination with our developing country partners, a refocused research agenda will also shape partnerships with other donors and the international and US-based research communities.

Though the research goals under FTF are ambitious, the magnitude of food insecurity worldwide demands coordinated and focused efforts to improve agricultural productivity for smallholder farm families in the developing world. Research aligned with this strategy will help to ensure the promise of Feed the Future, by science and technology being strategically directed and deployed towards achieving the Millennium Development Goal of reducing poverty and hunger.

****

PART ONE. INTRODUCTION AND ANALYTICAL BASIS

The Challenge

The President's Global Hunger and Food Security Initiative, titled "Feed the Future (FTF)", has the overarching goal of sustainably reducing global poverty and hunger (www.feedthefuture.gov). Providing sufficient food to the world's growing population will require a 70 percent increase in agricultural production by 2050, according to the Food and Agriculture Organization of the United Nations. To meet this food security challenge under constraints of limited agricultural land availability and increased climatic variability, the world will need to support and develop scientific and technological innovations that increase agricultural productivity in an environmentally sound manner while improving the availability of nutritious foods The food price spikes of 2006-2008 and that are resurfacing today underscore the fragility of global food security, with recent estimates that nearly a billion people are food insecure (Shapouri 2010). While the causes were many, the underlying challenges are clear: the world cannot achieve the Millennium Development Goals (http://www.un.org/millenniumgoals/) of reducing poverty and hunger when the growth of agricultural productivity and income stagnates or is otherwise insufficient.

It is predicted that in the coming decades the global population will increase by almost half with nearly all the growth occurring in developing regions of the world where hunger and poverty are already widespread. Thus, the world's producers will need to provide food for an additional 3 billion people, in many cases with less land per person, increased competition for scarce water and land resources, and under less predictable circumstances due to increased climatic variability (Bruinsma 2009; Royal Society 2009). To meet this food security challenge, the world, led by the United States, will need to rely on scientific and technological innovations resulting from rapid advances in both biophysical and information sciences that can be linked with local knowledge, environmental conditions, farming and changing dietary habits.

The Opportunity

New technologies, new management practices, and improved policies generated by research are key drivers of growth in agricultural productivity. Increased productivity means that producers can provide more (crops, livestock, dairy, eggs, poultry, fish, fiber, etc.) at lower cost thereby providing income growth for producers as well as income benefits for consumers due to increased purchasing power. The poor and food insecure populations benefit the most from such growth, since they spend the greatest proportion of their incomes on food. Income not required for purchasing or growing food can then be dedicated to education, health and re-invested in productive enterprise. On a larger scale, the multiplication of this process creates substantial economic linkages through demand for locally produced goods and services. Collectively, these growth processes have been shown repeatedly to be the most effective method for reducing poverty in low-income developing countries. Importantly, to ensure these benefits reach women, new research will focus on technologies and practices that address the constraints of women producers.

The greatest social benefits accrue to scientific discoveries with wide applicability. In agricultural research for development, plant breeding and genetics have generated the greatest impacts when accompanied by investments which have led to their adoption. For example, the short-stature but high-yielding Green Revolution varieties of wheat and rice, combined with fertilizer use and improved water management, enabled farmers to double and triple yields. Through enabling policy environments, effective diffusion of information through extension systems to farmers, and strengthened seed systems, these varieties have been adopted and improved upon over hundreds of millions of acres across the developing world, generating billions of dollars worth of food and income every year. Yet it is important to note that the gains are fragile since pests and diseases keep evolving; in other instances, gains have been much less due to a range of either biophysical or socio-economic factors. Thus, research must continue to generate new technologies and practices that sustain and build on past gains, while also developing approaches that help meet the needs of areas where advances have lagged.

Research to enhance agricultural productivity must also consider impacts on the natural environment, which is challenging given the greater uncertainty in agricultural productivity due to climate change. There is increasing evidence that continued research investment can sustain growth in agricultural productivity while conserving natural resources, thereby enhancing food security and incomes, and reducing poverty (Box 1). This requires the adaptation of global and regional research advances to local conditions, integrating soil, water and landscape in the context of environmental services and non-food security objectives.

Box 1. Sustainable Intensification: Increasing Productivity while Sustaining Natural Resources and the Environment

Agricultural productivity gains that reduce poverty and hunger and strengthen food security must be environmentally sound if the progress they drive is to be of a lasting nature. Soil and water conservation, energy and fertilizer efficiency and appropriate land use—all of these must be taken into account in a systems-level resource management strategy that underpins and sustains productivity gains. Non-agricultural uses often depend on shared environmental services and rely on sound stewardship of natural resources by the agricultural sector.

Direct benefits: At the heart of the Feed the Future strategy, the concept of 'sustainable intensification' encompasses scientific and information inputs with assessment of environmental impacts, at the point of the productive enterprise as well as upstream and downstream. Global research efforts are integrated into systems approaches that explicitly address natural resources. Major environmental benefits can go hand–in–hand with productivity enhancements:

(i) Conservation agriculture practices are revolutionizing agriculture in South Asia—improving soil fertility and raising organic matter content, saving water and energy, resulting in a more climate-resilient system while providing higher incomes for smallholder families.

(ii) In Southern Africa, new research-based agro-forestry systems for conserving soil and water through the use of nitrogen-fixing trees are spreading rapidly. In Southern Africa, 300,000 farm families have adopted these approaches, leading to maize yields that reach 4 tons/hectare, as well as improved soil water holding capacity, while avoiding excessive fertilizer application.

Indirect benefits: Sustainable intensification of land well suited to agriculture also provides important indirect environmental benefits. Evenson and Rosegrant (2003) estimated that CGIAR and national program crop germplasm improvement efforts improved crop yields so that 15-20 million additional hectares did not need to be brought into production to feed a growing population. Thus, with these productivity gains from the results and application of international agricultural research, forests, wetlands, hillsides and other biodiversity rich habitat were spared from being brought into agricultural production. Further, research on alternatives to slash–and–burn agriculture is offering new approaches that effectively reduce incentives to convert forests to agricultural land.

Record of Achievement

International agricultural research stands out as one of the best of all development investments. Its impacts are achieved, day in and day out, by virtue of both increased incomes for smallholders, increased demands for goods and services in the rural economy, and large spillover benefits to urban enterprises and consumers. Smallholder productivity gains in key staples and livestock have been shown to be extremely effective means to reduce poverty. Farm-level growth fuels demand for locally produced goods and services, generating off-farm employment opportunities and broad-based economic growth (Timmer 2005).

Consumers experience even greater gains from increased productivity in staple crops. By reducing real prices for widely consumed staple foods, poor people in particular will benefit. The impact of reduced real food prices on families who devote up to 60 percent of their incomes for staple foods cannot be underestimated (WDR 2008). By reducing the proportion of income spent on food, families have more resources to devote to education, health care and re-investment in other productive enterprises.

Box 2: Research, infrastructure, and knowledge lead to productivity gains.

Investing in agricultural research today reduces poverty in the future even in the face of increasing food demands. However, it is crucial that research is linked to other agricultural investments (extension, markets, infrastructure) to actually increase agricultural productivity and contribute to reductions in hunger and poverty. Agricultural productivity has risen in many developing countries, mostly as a result of investments in agricultural research combined with improved human capital and rural infrastructure. As research collapsed in the 1990s due to competing development priorities and declining investments, agricultural productivity growth rates in developing countries became much lower than those achieved in developed countries. Through the application of science, knowledge and related rural investments, the declining trends in productivity growth can be reversed and significant gains obtained in crop yields and cost efficiency in production.

For example, average maize yields in North America have reached 10 metric tons/hectare, while 2 tons/hectare is currently achieved in sub-Saharan Africa. Average rice yields in Southern Asia now exceed 3 tons/hectare, still well below half of the average yields in North America (FAOSTAT). However, significant gains in productivity cannot be achieved without the required investments in research to expand yield potential, and the necessary investments to ensure that the new technology is adapted and adopted by local farmers who also use sound crop, water and soil management practices.

Ex-post: Looking at the impact of the CGIAR system alone, Evenson and Rosegrant (2003) estimated that, absent impacts from CGIAR research, world food and feed grain prices would have been 18-21 percent higher, with huge negative effects on poor consumers. Food consumption per capita in the developing world would be 5 percent less, and 7 percent less in the poorest regions, leading to increased levels of hunger, poverty and malnutrition. As many as 15 million additional children, primarily in South Asia and Africa, would be malnourished. As more than half of all early childhood deaths in the developing world are directly related to malnutrition, the potential contributions of global agricultural research to reducing child undernutrition, when well targeted to advance health and nutrition goals, is great. Many additional research-derived impacts have been documented, for example, disease resistance in sorghum, groundnuts, and beans resulted from Collaborative Research Support Programs (CRSPs) research benefiting farmers in developing

11

countries and the US. Further, research advances in the US, such as the famous Norin10 cross by USDA-ARS researchers, led to the development of semi-dwarf wheat varieties spawning the Green Revolution.

Ex-ante: Economic analysis can quantify the impacts from past research investments. It is also extremely useful in assessing the potential impact of future research investments, and in fact is used widely in both developed and developing countries to consider future investment strategies. The example in Figure 1, taken from the CGIAR's Global Rice Science Platform (GRiSP) proposal (2010), posits that a $40 million annual investment (by several donors) in rice research for South Asia, as well as complementary efforts and investments by national and local partners, would result in aggregate discounted gross annual benefits for the South Asia subregion of about $4.4 billion by 2035. The same analysis also points out that the benefits resulting from CGIAR research arise as a result of investments along the entire value chain, underscoring the point that a range of research and related efforts are required to make and sustain gains over time.

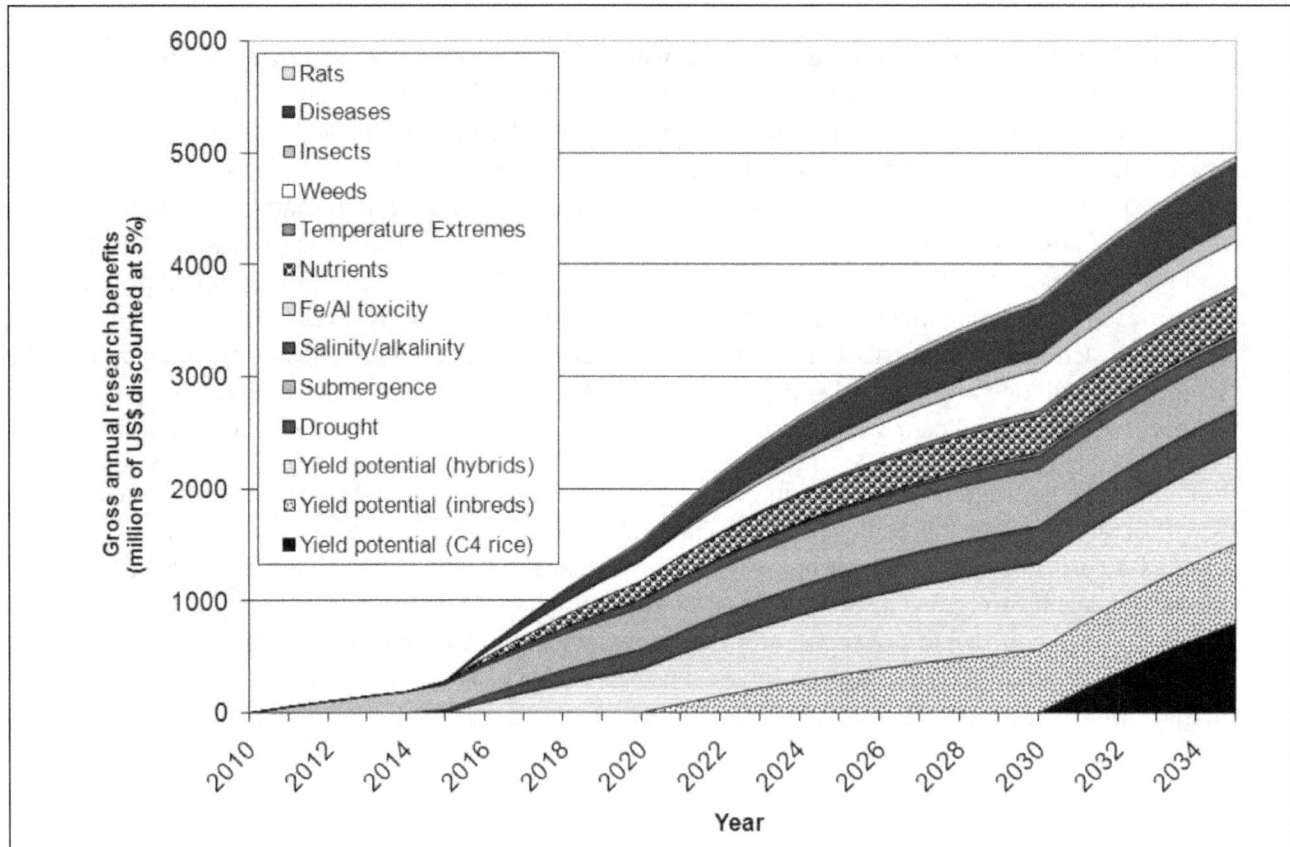

Figure 1. Ex-Ante Analysis Example: Expected Impacts from Rice Research in South Asia.

This graph indicates that of the 29.9 percent increase in net rice production by 2035, productivity growth specifically attributable to research investments account for 13.6 percent. Discounted attributable benefits of $32.4 billion would be generated from $1.0 billion in investment by 2035. (GRiSP 2010

Conceptual Framework: Research Economies of Scale, Spillovers and Timeframe:

In conceptual terms, the greatest impact comes from research outputs that not only have wide applicability, as indicated above, but moreover are of an "illuminating nature." These may include various scientific discoveries such as major breakthroughs in genetic research, which in addition to widespread applicability, also result in significant gains due to spillover impacts when appropriately adapted and adopted (Figure 2). The benefits from such research projects continue to accrue over many decades. However, these activities require substantial fixed investments in laboratories and other infrastructure, which may be difficult for developing countries to provide. Economies of scale are associated with fundamental biological and molecular research activities. In contrast, adaptive research activities designed to address specific problems are associated with lower economies of scale. These research programs may require smaller level of investments and their impact can be limited to a specific region or crops/livestock. But adaptive research (lower left in grid of Figure 2) has bigger immediate impacts on poverty and hunger alleviation within a specific location or population.

Figure 2: A conceptual framework for differing types of research investments, highlighting trade-offs related to the scope of a research effort.

Adaptive research generally builds on more broadly applicable or more basic advances—thus the two streams of effort are linked and interdependent, as indicated in Figure 2. Figure 2 maps the intersection between the potential scale, spillovers and timeframe of various types of research designed to reduce poverty and hunger. Activities in the top right sector of the grid in Figure 2 represent the initial portion of a research pipeline. Innovations and breakthroughs such as genome mapping and identification of disease resistant genes that occur at this stage feed into the center sector of grid, where the genetic breakthroughs are adapted to local varieties and breeds. Actual adoption of new varieties by farmers occurs in the bottom-left sector of grid, E. Information from sectors B and E feed into data analysis in sector D and agro-climatic models in sector C. Results from these analyses influence research, and investment decisions move along all three diagonal stages, A, B, and E, creating a feedback loop which is essential for continued high-impact research and development.

For example, a drought resistant variety of maize in the research pipeline may be in the process of being adopted. The enabling market and policy environment, supported through social science research to better understand information dissemination systems, farmer decision making processes and policy/market factors necessary for an enabling environment, can facilitate the availability, deployment, and adoption of this new variety in suitable areas. This can also provide evaluation and feedback later regarding the success of this new technology. Strong extension capabilities will allow this new technology to be properly adopted. Moreover, information available through agro-climatic modeling may improve the efficacy of the deployment of this new maize variety into different types of agronomic conditions in a country or a region, as well as provide a means of forecasting future food availability and assessing the food security situation for the region.

Understanding of this context led to three strategic decisions under the Feed the Future Initiative (FTF) which are outlined here.

- **Balance High Spillover/High Capital with Low Spillover/Low Capital Research.** *FTF* will use a portfolio approach selecting research opportunities along a continuum to balance research time horizons and scale of impact. On one end of that continuum, there are global scientific research opportunities that are associated with greater investment needs for longer-term research that can result in broad-based benefits (research strategy outlined here and funded from the International Public Goods research funds of the FTF Initiative). At the other end of the continuum is research requiring less investment and provides short-term results but which have narrower, more localized benefits (funded through other parts of the FTF initiative, especially country-level programs). The economies of scale associated with fundamental scientific research will be exploited through collaboration with national and international research agencies, particularly the US Land Grant University CRSPs and CGIAR centers. Collaborating with the CGIAR Research Programs and CRSPs will facilitate investments in basic scientific research designed to benefit developing countries where it would not be cost-effective to finance such capital-intensive research facilities. Programs with benefits limited to countries or regions only (i.e., less spillover potential) will engage funding from country-level or regional programs.

- **Balance Short and Longer Term International Public Goods Research.** The USG strategy will identify on-going research where additional funds can accelerate benefits. Given the length of time required from inception of research to completion and diffusion to users, scientific research investments must be designed as a pipeline which yields short, intermediate and longer-term outputs. In some cases ongoing research projects designed to yield scientific discovery with-high-spillover potential may achieve the objective in a shorter time period with the infusion of additional resources, particularly when this is in regard to dissemination and adoption of existing technologies (see below). By generating stronger linkages with national-level programs envisioned in this strategy, impacts from and demand for appropriate research-based innovations will also increase.

- **Balance Research, Extension, Policy and Information.** Thus, the USG will maximize the impact of its global research investments with FTF country-level complementary investments in systems level research, extension services, policy analysis, capacity building, and information systems made at the country level. These interventions can accelerate the dissemination of research into farmers' fields and provide feedback to researchers. In light of the nearer-term horizon and geographic focus of the country-level interventions, funding from national and regional-level programs will be vital to the full implementation of these approaches.

Implications for Global Research

Major breakthroughs are increasingly generated from basic biological research and its molecular tools. Today, researchers in both the public and private sectors use a range of gene-based approaches to work on new traits such as drought tolerance and increased nutrient use efficiency coupled with the more traditional traits such as disease and pest resistance. Such research can lead to increased food productivity which reduces risk and can benefit farmers in both developed and developing regions ("dual applicability" or spillover). Generating international public goods (e.g., new or improved crop traits, livestock vaccines, policy innovations) that are relevant across large areas is a key focus of the global research strategy.

In the context of the CGIAR and US Land Grant University CRSPs for example, core breeding capabilities in major staples have generated the largest returns (with extensive spillover to the United States and other developed regions). However, integration of component technologies into production systems must also occur and requires adaptive research. Adaptive research activities are designed to address specific problems and incorporate biophysical, socio-cultural and economic considerations in the development of approaches to address the problem. These research programs usually require smaller levels of investment with impact more limited to a specific region or crop/livestock/fish production system. Bridging global science and research serving the needs of poorer, smallholder producers requires improved human and institutional capacity through substantial fixed investments in science assets such as staff, laboratories and research infrastructure including equipment, greenhouses, and field sites.

Ultimately, we need scientific breakthroughs, international public goods research, and adaptive research to impact food security. All three sectors need to interact, exchanging analyses and other information to link real-world problems with solutions that can be generated all along the research continuum from the seemingly more esoteric basic genomics research to the farmer's field. All three research sectors share a problem-solving orientation, and, when connected, form an ideal continuum of purpose-driven research.

Whole of Government and Strategic Partnerships

The strategy adopts a new whole of government approach to leverage the existing competencies in each USG agency toward the common goals of reducing poverty and hunger. The Department of State, the U.S. Agency for International Development (USAID) and the U.S. Department of Agriculture (USDA) are joining forces to design and implement the *Feed the Future* Research Strategy. Other relevant USG agencies, such as the National Science Foundation, the National

Institutes of Health, and others will also be involved where they can bring their resources to bear on FTF goals. While the focus of this strategy is global research, to ensure a demand-driven program that has impact in the FTF Focus Countries we are also coordinating with multilateral institutions, USG missions in countries, national and regional research institutions and other USG agencies such as the Millennium Challenge Corporation (MCC).

Sustainable Intensification

The *Feed the Future* research strategy will be underpinned by the philosophy of sustainable intensification whereby science, knowledge, best resource management practices, improved inputs and improved policies and incentive structures will be used to reduce yield gaps in developing countries taking into consideration environmental concerns, soil fertility, and the natural resource base. The sustainability of crop and animal production systems relies on the stewardship and enhancement of all available natural and human resources, particularly when used in systems that achieve productivity as well as environmental and social goals.

Purpose-Driven Research

Research priorities for *Feed the Future* emerged from extensive analysis of the geographic distribution of child undernutrition and poverty and the farming systems of the poor in these areas. Figures 3 and 4 show clearly that poverty and malnutrition are most concentrated in South Asia, the highlands of East and Central Africa, a broad swath of Southern Africa and the dryland savannas and Sahel region of West Africa. The analysis targeted those farming systems with the greatest concentration of poverty and child undernutrition, and reviewed research opportunities to yield improvements in food availability, accessibility, and utilization. Given the multiple pathways by which agriculture can be harnessed to improve nutrition (World Bank, 2007), we specifically looked for research opportunities that would improve availability, access and utilization of high quality micronutrient-dense diets among women and children.

We recognize that in many of these regions where undernutrition and poverty are prevalent, the poor depend on agriculture for their livelihoods and we considered the range of pathways by which agriculture can improve nutrition and reduce poverty. We analyzed a broad array of factors - biophysical, social, economic, and policy-related - that can impact agriculture-led productivity growth and mapped these to national-level priorities defined by governments of FTF Focus Countries. The range of factors that were identified range from commodity-specific production constraints including technology adoption issues to farming systems-level constraints. Biophysical constraints to production and along the value chain were defined based on a series of consultations and analyses involving producers, farmer organizations, private sector agribusiness, NGOs, researchers and extension workers. Country-identified priorities generally focused on specific commodities as opposed to specific biophysical constraints to production or constraints along the value chain for those commodities, thus literature review and stakeholder consultations identified the key researchable topics for these priorities. Constraints were overlaid with the major agro-ecosystems noted above, so that the most important problems became evident. In addition to a focus on biophysical constraints to production and value chains, the analysis examined literature on the social and policy environments, where possible, of areas with the greatest levels of poverty and undernutrition. Common themes arose across major agro-ecosystems such as constraints to farmer uptake of new technologies and water policy issues. Researchable problems of an international public goods nature were discerned from problems where other approaches were more appropriate. In many cases, more than one approach is needed, and in other cases, solutions may be known and continued research will not contribute significantly to addressing the issue. Expert judgments were drawn from a broad range of strategy development processes including those of the CGIAR, Global Forum for Agriculture Research (GFAR), scientific academies and others. Based on a broad set of expert analyses and consultations, researchable constraints emerged.

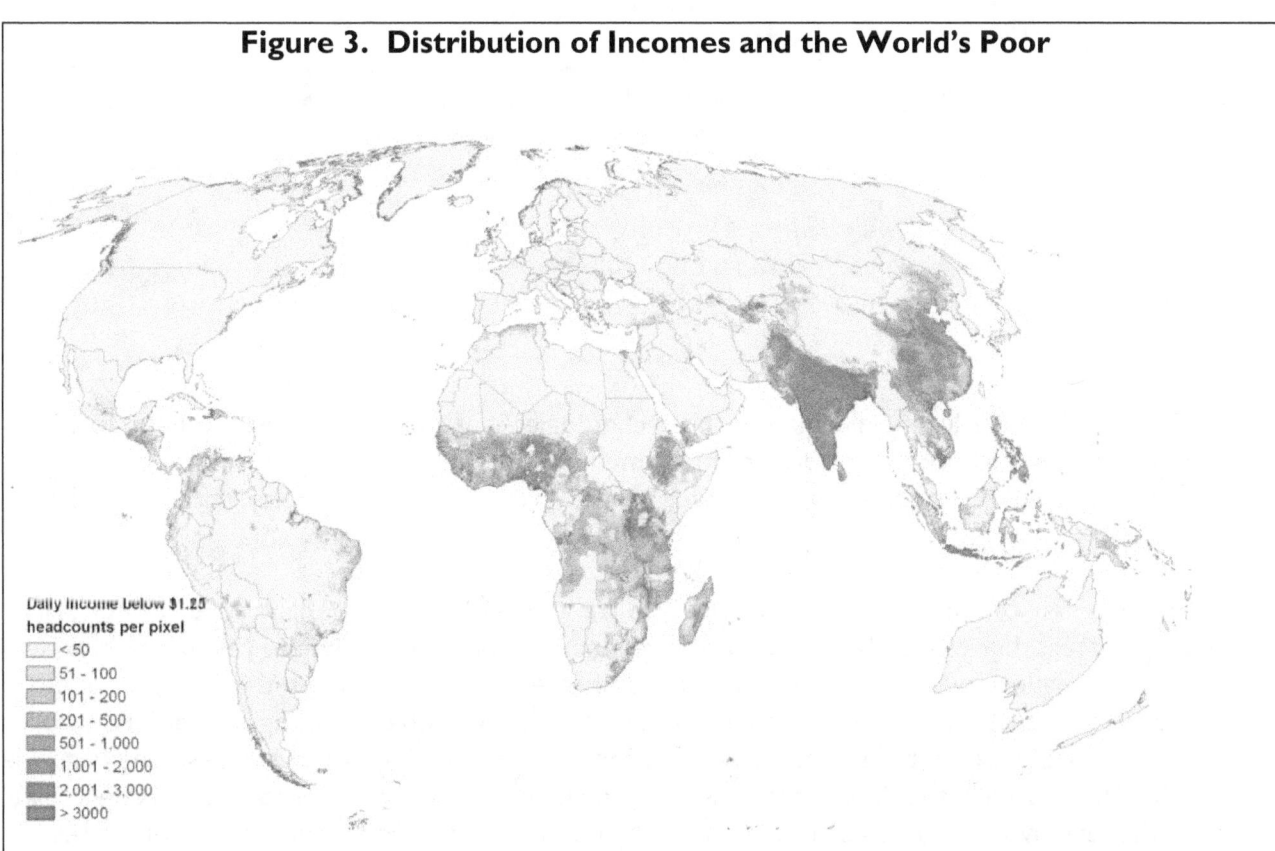

Figure 3. Distribution of Incomes and the World's Poor

Daily income below $1.25 headcounts per pixel

- < 50
- 51 - 100
- 101 - 200
- 201 - 500
- 501 - 1,000
- 1,001 - 2,000
- 2,001 - 3,000
- > 3000

Several major agricultural systems are home to many of the world's poor and hungry. Distribution of poverty coincides with major agricultural production systems, highlighting agriculture as key to gains in both incomes and food security.

Source: CGIAR Strategy and Results Framework Spatial Analysis Team, Stan Wood et al. (CGIAR, World Bank, RIMISP, and other resources)

Source: CGIAR Strategy and Results Framework Spatial Analysis Team, Stan Wood et al. (CGIAR, World Bank, RIMISP, and other resources)

Research outputs including information and technologies that solve problems also need to be assessed in a framework that prioritizes investments most likely to generate impacts including the goal of increased incomes for women as well as men producers, using the key criteria listed in Box 3.

A large number of candidate research priorities were generated in this analysis. For any priority-setting process, but especially for research investments supported by limited resources, choices need to be made about comparative advantages of research partners and the most appropriate approach for collaboration, which depends upon the type of problem-solving needed. For more upstream problem-oriented research, the approach needs to be highly focused resulting in greater depth. The approach should also increase the probability that adequate resources will be available over the lengthy time frame required to achieve the milestones. For research that integrates multiple streams of international public goods (IPGs) into broadly applicable products or outputs, a broader range of investments may be required, reflecting the fact that the best of solutions often depend on relevant technologies and innovations.

An example would be a breeding program aimed primarily at developing resistance to a particular problem but which incorporates selection for a number of additional traits crucial to the productivity of the crop in a variety of environments and additional traits of interest to farmers and consumers. Finally, further downstream application-level research may include approaches that depend on a range of components (such as improved crops and fertilizers, increased understanding of farmer decision making processes/risk tolerance/aversion to new technologies, and others) each of which makes a contribution to solving a focused problem possessing multiple facets.

Box 3. Scale and Impact: Criteria for Research Investment

While potential impact and scalability and spillover are critical for global research, a more detailed analysis guides investments. The following are the key criteria that guided the selection of research priorities for the *Feed the Future* initiative:

- Relevance to poverty, women and children and reduced vulnerability objectives

- Likelihood of success: Technical merit, clear pathways for deployment/adoption

- Cost/Benefit: Estimated cost to develop technology vs. potential returns in terms of impacts.

- Economic sustainability for producers/adopters

- Natural resources sustainability: water, soil, ecosystem and climate change.

- Institutional sustainability/impact on capacity: engagement of national and regional partners

- Time Frame: timeline, milestones

- Risks: potential impacts on vulnerable groups, environment or breakdown in key pathways

---

Identifying research opportunities that can address biophysical constraints to production or social/policy environments that constrain access to food yielded priorities that address both systems-level issues as well as factors relevant to an individual commodity and its value chain. While commodity-specific research will target constraints to production and effective value chains for specific crops and livestock, FTF will also invest in research to identify pathways for technology impact, including understanding farmer decision making and information dissemination to ensure that investments shepherd new technologies through the pipeline from laboratory to farm to the broadest number of farmers, particularly women and poor farmers. Further, opportunities to integrate research activities to improve nutrition impacts will be prioritized.

Systems-level research priorities include issues related to the biophysical, policy and social contexts, particularly related to gender equity and the distribution of benefits from agricultural research. Market and trade policy research are integral components of strategic decision-making to optimize the benefits of technology deployment and to minimize unforeseen adverse consequences. Finally, each research theme has an integrated priority assessment process to inform subsequent decision-making regarding investment strategies and resource allocation. Thus, as new information becomes available, it can be integrated into the decision making process to improve research investments.

From this overlay of criteria, constraints and research opportunities together, three general categories of priorities emerged:

- **Advancing the Productivity Frontier:** A focus on breeding and genetics for major crops and livestock and vaccine development to increase yield potential and provide solutions for major biotic and abiotic production constraints which ultimately will increase incomes and reduce risks for agricultural producers – both women and men. To more effectively integrate the use of these technologies among poor farmers, research under this theme will also address socio-behavioral factors and incentive structures/policy context related to technology adoption.

- **Transforming Key Production Systems:** Focusing on agricultural systems where the poor are concentrated, global research resources will join with national and regional efforts so that increases in systems-level productivity are achieved while addressing environmental sustainability. This will be accomplished by integrating available technologies and best practices, in addition to ongoing implementation of lessons learned through analysis of the social and policy context with particular attention to interaction effects of multiple technologies/approaches/policy innovations on farmer incomes and child nutrition.

- **Enhancing Nutrition and Food Safety:** This theme emphasizes the importance of ensuring that agricultural systems contribute to nutrition and health goals. This theme will focus on agricultural research opportunities to improve availability and access to a high quality diet, particularly for women and young children. Through targeted research in the natural and social sciences, we will focus agricultural systems on improving nutrition through diversification of production systems, enhancing dietary diversity and nutrient density of foods and reducing postharvest losses. This theme will also improve utilization of food through attention to food safety challenges with a focus on reducing contaminants in the food supply. Research priorities in this theme are integrally linked to the first two themes thereby leveraging those investments to ensure the dual focus on improving nutrition and reducing poverty.

These three streams join in the concept of "Sustainable Intensification" in which research (such as technologies and best management practices) and non-research inputs (such as fertilizer, quality seed, water, energy, market information, and others) come together with improved access to markets to increase productivity, enhance environmental sustainability, reduce risk, and encourage producers to increase investments to agricultural production. Research is designed with an eye towards the roles of women and men as producers and consumers, to ensure that the new systems and component technologies meet household livelihood and nutritional needs. Sustainable agriculture intensification addresses both economic and environmental requirements, contributing generally to substantial positive impacts (such as increased soil fertility and organic matter content, reduced energy use, enhanced watershed and reduced soil erosion).

Indirect impacts of sustainable intensification can also be substantial. For example, by intensifying production and profitability in more resilient agriculture-appropriate environs, more fragile and/or sensitive environments can benefit from reduced pressure from use for agriculture (see Box 1).

PART TWO. RESEARCH THEMES

I. Advancing the Productivity Frontier

Yield potential is defined as the productivity of crops or livestock when sufficient nutrients and water are provided and pests, diseases, weeds and other stresses are absent or minimal. Food security research to increase productivity above current levels under optimal conditions bridges increases in yield potential with yield gains associated with stress-tolerance. Priorities will be focused on obtaining optimal productivity on farms through biophysical and social/economic research. The goal of this research theme is to reduce risk for farmers and increase availability of high quality foods, particularly key crops and livestock produced by smallholders, including cereal and root/tuber staple crops, legumes, fish, cattle and poultry. The research will aim to achieve on-farm productivity levels equivalent to those found under more ideal conditions such as in-country experiment stations. FTF research will invest in the development of metrics and methodologies needed to measure crop system productivity vis-à-vis resource utilization (water, nutrients, and energy). FTF research will also examine factors that inform farmer decision making related to adoption of technology/innovative management approaches as well as increase our understanding of and development of effective information dissemination systems to reach a broad array of farmers, including women and poor farmers. Analyses related to climate change, water, and emerging pests and diseases will be factored into this research theme.

For crops, the strategy will focus on constraints known to severely impact availability of staple crops including biotic (pests, diseases) and abiotic (drought, heat and other environmental) stress factors. The emphasis will be on genetic enhancement to overcome such constraints, as well as assuring the conservation and availability of the genetic resource base, including crop, invertebrate, and microbial genetic resources, which underpin research to enhance agricultural productivity in the developing world. Research on cereals and root/tuber/banana staples has been prioritized for three basic reasons: the importance of these crops in the diets of smallholder farmers and low-income consumers; in meeting local, regional and international market demands; and the demonstrated ability that high productivity of widely-grown and consumed staples reduces poverty.

Research on livestock, poultry and fish has been included because of growing demand for these foods and the demonstrated importance of animal source foods on preventing undernutrition in children. We will target problems in this sector to reduce poverty and hunger especially focusing on the needs of women, in their roles as both producers and consumers. Following are key areas of investment, with illustrative examples. Data from unpublished ex-ante analyses are included to illustrate the potential gains from different research investments.

To complement the focus on crop and livestock productivity, we will also emphasize the importance of key socio-behavioral, economic, and policy factors that impact on-farm productivity relating to technology adoption. Particular attention will be focused on farmer-level considerations to the adoption of technology and the development and evaluation of differentiated extension models to increase the availability and utilization of innovative management approaches and new technologies which contribute to improved productivity of crops and livestock among women and poor farmers. Research on extension will include analyses of information dissemination and uptake, including development and evaluation of appropriate information and communication technologies (ICT).

Crop Improvement

Reducing risks from pests and disease. Smallholder farmers rely on staple crop production for both income and household food security. Yield losses associated with pests and diseases are significant and ameliorating these will reduce risk for farmers. Focusing our research strategy on the crops and constraints with broadest significance across production systems, we identified the following research areas as examples where global investments can enable us to forge partnerships with national and regional research institutions, the private sector, public-private partnership organizations, and NGOs for technology generation and dissemination to overcome these constraints:

- *Cassava mosaic and brown streak virus:* African cassava mosaic virus is one of the most widespread diseases affecting cassava which, along with maize, is one of that continent's most important food staples. Brown streak, a new and devastating disease that damages the cassava plant's root, rending them inedible and worthless, is spreading across East Africa.

- *Maize streak virus, borers, gray leaf spot:* Maize is the most important food crop across wide areas of Africa, but it suffers from a suite of pests and diseases that decrease yields and increase risks for smallholder, low-income producers.

- *Striga:* One of the most devastating parasitic weeds afflicting global agriculture is striga, a weed that attacks fields of sorghum, maize and cowpea in Africa.

- *Insect-resistant cowpea:* West Africa's farmers produce more than 3 million tons of cowpea each year, providing critical protein to low-income groups (FAOSTAT). The crop is extremely susceptible to insect attack and requires frequent spraying with pesticides, and *Maruca* pod borers alone can cause losses up to 80 percent of yield (Coulibaly 2008).

- *Wheat stem rust:* A half-century of durable resistance to wheat stem rust has broken down in the wake of a new and virulent race of stem rust known as Ug99. An epidemic of this race, which attacks 80-90 percent of wheat varieties currently grown (FAO 2008), could threaten food security across East Africa, the Middle East and South Asia and eventually cause major losses in U.S. agriculture.

- *Potato Late Blight:* The cause of the Irish potato famine is still a major threat to livelihoods and food security in many mid- and high-elevation areas of Africa, Asia and Latin America, causing an estimated $2.75 billion in losses each year in these regions (CIP 2010).

Crop resistance to heat, drought, salinity and flood. Climate change is increasing the importance of adapting multiple staple crops to heat and drought stress tolerance, while submergence tolerance will be critical for rice production in some of Asia's poorest communities. Such adaptations represent key means of reducing smallholder risks, helping buffer farm productivity and incomes from frequent shocks due to weather. Key examples include:

- *Flood-tolerance in rice*: Submergence affects some 20 million hectares of rice in Asia and Africa, causing annual losses that can reach $1 billion (IRRI 2010a).

- *Drought-tolerant rice for Asia*: Drought affects more than 23 million hectares of rainfed rice in South and Southeast Asia (IRRI 2010b). In parts of eastern India, severe droughts (usually once every five years) cause losses that average 40 percent (IRRI 2010b). These drought-prone rice producing areas are home to a significant number of Asia's absolute poor.

- *Heat-tolerant wheat*: Wheat yields in the Indo-Gangetic plains – which account for 15% of global wheat production - are at risk from high temperatures, with estimates that 51% of the region will be reclassified as a heat-stressed production environment (Ortiz 2008).

- *Drought-tolerant maize for Africa*: Millions of African farm families face unpredictable weather that hampers production of maize, their staple crop and most important food.

Expanding yield potential of crops. Discovery research aimed at yield breakthroughs can be adapted to crops grown in developing countries and their environments, but most such research will be supported with higher-risk research resources from NSF, USDA and other sources. In some instances, we will work to deploy available tools and technologies to top priority food security-related concerns, for example:

- *Hybrid wheat and rice*: Hybrid rice can boost yield advantages 15-20 percent (Tran 2004). At the same time, more acres are being planted with hybrid rice, increasing from just 0.8 million hectares in 2001/2002 to 3 million ha in 2008 in Asia outside China (Tran 2004, IFPRI 2009).

- *Photosynthetic efficiency gains*: Researchers are exploring new means of increasing the efficiency of solar energy conversion in crops that are most important for the world's food security (Royal Society 2009). This is an area where longer-horizon research holds great promise for increasing yields.

Improved resource use efficiency of crops. Lack of soil fertility continues to reduce crop production for poor farmers and reductions in water availability is increasingly challenging production; thus, increased efficiency of staple crops will be critical for farmers to ensure continued and increasing levels of production in a changing environment. Key examples where new investments can make a significant impact include:

- *Nitrogen-use efficient rice for Africa*

- *Enhanced biological nitrogen fixation in legumes*: Part of a broader effort to boost productivity of leguminous crops, this advanced research will target efforts to raise the amount of nitrogen fixed by bean and other grain legume crops.

- *Water-use efficiency*: Advanced research in plant physiology and genetics is exploring a range of mechanisms that would enable crops to become more water-use efficient.

- *Water, energy, and greenhouse gas metrics*: Research in developing methodologies for diagnosing crop system productivity with respect to water usage, energy usage, biodiversity conservation, and greenhouse gases emissions as well as information management tools will be necessary in order to further target ongoing investments in areas of highest potential to positively impact resource usage, land use management, and climate change mitigation.

Strengthen the genetic resource base. Underpinning all the crop improvement efforts is continued collaboration between USDA's National Plant Germplasm System (NPGS), USAID-supported CGIAR gene banks (the world's largest collections) and the Global Crop Diversity Trust, which will ensure greater efficiency and coordination in assuring global future food security. As availability of microbial and invertebrate genetic resources is critical for improving plant and animal productivity and environmental sustainability of production systems, we include attention to research on preservation, characterization, and use of *Rhizobia* and other relevant microbial and invertebrate genetic resources in this research area.

Animal Source Food (livestock, fish and poultry)

Just as in the case of crops, extensive research has shown that increasing productivity of livestock and poultry in smallholder settings can lead to substantial impacts on poverty, as well as providing improved nutrition through enhanced availability of meat, fish, dairy and eggs. Research priorities may address: 1) the control of infectious diseases of livestock, some of which are zoonoses (infectious diseases that affect animals as well as humans) and thus threaten human health as well; 2) developing management approaches for improved aquaculture productivity, 3) improved quality animal feeds (for livestock, poultry, and fish), and 4) livestock genetics and breeding for improved productivity. USDA and others in the U.S. research community are well poised to contribute to expanded research efforts to combat several important diseases by developing vaccines and better diagnostic tools.

Infectious Diseases of Cattle in SSA. Livestock and their products offer a powerful pathway out of poverty for millions of smallholder farmers and pastoralists. Moreover, for pastoralists livestock may be the main food source since they convert grasses and shrubbery to protein in regions were these are the only available crops. Infectious livestock diseases feature high among the constraints faced by poor farmers and vaccines have the power to eradicate disease. However, development of vaccines is a high risk / high return and long-term undertaking, which during the research phase is assisted and accelerated by knowledge generation occurring in other disciplines of biological and physical sciences as well as technical know-how from the private pharmaceutical sector. Recent priority setting efforts highlight the following needs and research opportunities:

- *Contagious bovine pleural pneumonia (CBPP)*: This is an example of a disease of cattle that has moved from North to South and is now considered to be one of the most damaging diseases of cattle in Africa, resulting in mortality of up to 50 percent of infected animals, and 100% morbidity in herds that had not previously been exposed (Thomson 2005).

- *East coast fever (theileriosis)*: A tick-borne disease that is frequently fatal (killing 90 percent of infected exotic breeds of cattle and more than 50 percent of indigenous breeds), East Coast Fever (ECF) is estimated to kill more than 1 million cattle annually (more than 1 animal every 30 seconds) (Di Giulio 2009), resulting in $160-250 million in economic losses (Spielman 2008).

- *Other diseases: Trypanosomiasis, Rift Valley Fever, Foot and Mouth Disease:* These diseases cause major losses or pose important trade obstacles.
  - Foot and Mouth Disease, while not endemic in the United States, it generally requires control in other countries to reduce the virus circulation of this highly contagious virus worldwide thus benefiting both developed and developing countries.

  - Trypanosomiasis, a tsetse fly transmitted protozoan, affects 10 million square kilometers in 36 African countries thus putting 50 million cattle at risk with 3 million cattle and 50,000 humans dying annually. The economic cost of trypanomiasis alone is $4.5 billion/year (AU-IBAR 2010).

  - Rift Valley Fever is a sporadic disease that, for 50% of humans experiencing its most severe form, is fatal. The disease leads to 100 percent abortion of infected pregnant sheep and the death of 90 percent of infected lambs (WHO 2010).

Aquaculture. Aquaculture, or "fish farming" is essential both for meeting food security objectives and for sustaining wild fish stocks and essential habitats, including coral reefs and mangroves. Sustainable aquaculture systems can relieve the pressure on more fragile systems, as well as provide livelihoods that are especially open to women as managers and entrepreneurs.

A key concern surrounding aquaculture relates to the introduction of species (such as *Tilapia spp.*) that can threaten indigenous fish breeds. Research investments that assess and integrate indigenous species hold out great promise for increasing incomes and nutrition while at the same time protecting key habitat. The opportunities are significant, especially given the specialization that occurs across species even within a small pond managed by low-income families. Further, research on improved management approaches with particular attention to environmental impacts (e.g. water quality/effluent) of different aquaculture production systems will be prioritized to improve the productivity and environmental sustainability of aquaculture in FTF Focus Countries. By linking species-level diversification with environmental and economic assessments, FTF sponsored research can lead to greater income and sustainability outcomes on farm, and benefit conservation efforts dependent on protected habitats in coral reefs and elsewhere.

Quality Animal Feed. Improved availability of quality animal feeds is critical to both aquatic animal and livestock productivity in many FTF Focus Countries. This research priority links with research in improvements of crop productivity and social science research on farmer-level considerations to ensure multi-use criteria are considered in the development of crops for food and feed.

Genetics & Breeding. Breeds of livestock including cattle, sheep, goats and poultry that are indigenous to particular regions of the world have enhanced disease resistance compared to breeds developed elsewhere. They also have greater capacity to survive in the hotter environments found in sub-Saharan Africa. However these indigenous breeds may be less productive than those developed in Europe and the United States. Key research opportunities include:

- Development of highly productive livestock and poultry through breeding and other technologies that have greater innate resistance to infectious diseases that occur in their local environments
- Development of fish breeds with higher feed conversion efficiency and disease resistance. Significant productivity enhancement from improved fish breeds will likely only occur after productivity increases are achieved from improved aquaculture management practices in target systems, thus aquatic animal breeding will be a second tier priority.
- Development of preservation technologies and policy studies for livestock and aquatic animal germplasm would ensure the long term resilience and usefulness of national and global germplasm collections.

Technology Adoption

This research area will include participatory approaches and address issues such as information systems that are effective and socially inclusive, with particular emphasis on identifying ways to build gender-sensitive systems of information dissemination to ensure broad access to information to enhance productivity. It would analyze incentive structures/policies and risk factors that impact decision-making processes among farmers.

- Development and evaluation of flexible and gender-sensitive extension models to increase availability and utilization of technologies and innovative management practices that enhance productivity of crops and livestock among diverse conditions and types of farmers, including women and poor farmers. Research on extension will include analyses of information dissemination, uptake, and sustainability, including development application and evaluation of appropriate information and communication technologies (ICT).

- Examination of factors – both farmer-level considerations (agro-ecological, social, cultural, and economic) and policies- that impact decision making processes among farmers is critical to developing an enabling environment at the local and national levels for farmers to realize increases in agricultural productivity. This research area will examine local, national, regional policy environments and structural/institutional factors that shape incentives for farmer adoption of new technologies or practices. It will also examine resource constraints, risk factors, and tradeoff considerations that influence farmer decision making processes.

Research Priorities Assessment & Evaluation

This targeted area would support research to provide for:

- Ongoing assessment of research priorities, investment strategies and resource allocation for the FTF focus areas. This will allow for timely modifications of research activities and resource allocations to respond to emerging threats to food security or to changes in the economic or institutional environments.

- Development of methods for evaluating FTF investments and developing improved, low-cost and effective tools and methods for impact assessment. This research will be focused on ensuring that the FTF research portfolio and the larger investments at the country level provide transformational change to developing country agriculture with an emphasis on reducing poverty and improving child nutrition.

II. Transforming Key Production Systems

Regional research and development programs will link global, regional and national partners to identify and invest through both research and non-research approaches critical to sustainable intensification of agricultural systems. Systems intensification will be based on both component technologies (often spearheaded at the global level) with eco-regional systems-level practices. Key researchable areas that will need to be integrated within the target systems include agronomy, soil fertility, water resource management, pest management, market access and policies. This research theme recognizes that the determinants of poverty and undernutrition are complex, interactive, and vary by geographic region, and that social, policy, economic, and biophysical contexts must be considered. They will influence not only whether and how new production practices and technologies are adopted, but also the sustainability of adopting new approaches, practices, and technologies. Each priority system will include the following areas of social science/policy research:

- o Systems level analyses of the socio-behavioral, economic and policy dimensions of multiple technologies/innovations and their interactions on outcomes of poverty and undernutrition

- o Research to understand decision making criteria and processes of diverse types of farmers operating with multiple goals and varying levels of access to key resources

- o Research on flexible and gender sensitive extension models to ensure that diverse groups of farmers benefit from these systems-approach strategies
- o Examination of the institutional/structural barriers, including policy context (e.g. water policy, market incentives, etc.), that shape access to resources linked to farmers' technology/innovation adoption and continued use

Production Systems Intensification

Working with FTF Focus Countries, we will identify priority systems for sustainable intensification. Combining systems-level and component technology approaches with a focus on gender-sensitive research needs, decision making factors, and structural/institutional barriers to technology adoption and continued use, we anticipate the following regions will emerge as high priority research and development objectives:

- *South Asia cereal-based systems*: Stretching from Pakistan to Bangladesh, this target region will integrate globally-funded research technologies at the level of regional system to assure productivity gains in the face of greater water resource competition and a warming climate. Research may emphasize:

  - o heat- and drought-tolerant rice and wheat
  - o rust-resistant wheat
  - o cold- and heat-tolerant grain legumes
  - o quality protein maize linked to dairy/poultry value chains
  - o nutrition-enhancing, high-value vegetable crops

- o conservation tillage

- o water, nutrient, and energy conserving practices

- o groundwater and water basin management research (policy and measurement/monitoring methodologies)

- *East Africa highland systems:* From Ethiopia through to the Great Lakes region, mid- and high-elevation systems suffer from nutrient depletion and a range of pests and diseases. Livestock are very important and competition for limited feed resources presents major challenges to sustainable intensification and soil fertility enhancement. Investments under consideration include:

  - o rust-resistant wheat

  - o drought- and streak-tolerant maize

  - o higher-productivity beans and other grain legumes

  - o disease-resistant potato and bananas

  - o virus-resistant cassava

  - o conservation agriculture practices

  - o intensified feed production for livestock

  - o large ruminant marketing systems

  - o practices to conserve water and soil

- *Southern and Eastern Africa maize-based systems:* Further south, from Tanzania across Zambia and Malawi down to Mozambique, at lower elevations and under drier conditions, maize is the defining crop for millions of food-insecure smallholders. Sustainable intensification equates with improving resilience in the face of frequent drought through improving soil moisture holding capacity and diversification for both fertility and income growth. The following research areas will address critical challenges and needs:

  - o drought-tolerant maize and sorghum

  - o higher-productivity grain legumes and oilseeds

  - o improving rice productivity in new and rehabilitated irrigation schemes as an alternative to dryland maize

  - o integration of indigenous vegetables and horticultural crops

  - o integration of nitrogen-fixing shrubs and trees

  - o small ruminant feed and marketing systems

  - o high-beta carotene, pest-resistant sweet potato

  - o disease-resistant cassava and banana in more humid areas

  - o water use efficiency traits in staple crops

  - o water management and conservation policies and practices

  - o fertilizer or nutrient management, policies, and practices

- *West African Sudano-Sahelian systems*: Encompassing a vast region from the Atlantic to Sudan, a wide belt shares a north-south rainfall gradient and closely integrated marketing of agricultural products in established trade corridors. Improved water management is at the heart of intensified systems in this region, along with attention to natural resource management in the context of pastoral systems, and crops adapted to heat, drought, diseases and pest and the appropriate integration of horticultural crops. Livestock feed is a major issue. The following areas will be emphasized:

  o drought- and pest-tolerant sorghum and millet

  o drought-, Striga, - and streak-tolerant maize

  o insect-resistant cowpea

  o disease and pest-resistant groundnut

  o integration of indigenous vegetables and horticultural crops

  o intensified animal feed production

  o in-field water catchment

  o livestock marketing systems

  o water management and conservation policies and practices

  o fertilizer or nutrient management, policies, and practices

  o natural resources management with emphasis on pastoral systems issues

Anticipated Impacts from Systems Research

South Asia is home to the first Sustainable Intensification program involving a combination of global, regional and bilateral Mission funding from USAID paired with a similar range of funding from the Bill and Melinda Gates Foundation. As in the case of productivity focused research, ex-ante analyses indicate that significant impacts can be achieved through sustainable intensification of agricultural production systems.

- *South Asia*: Based on ex ante analyses, the Cereal Systems Initiative for South Asia has set targets for the middle of the decade whereby sustainable intensification of wheat, rice and maize production will be achieved through better access to high quality seed and information and implementation of best management practices. It is estimated that this work can lead to yield increases of about ½ ton/ha on 5 million hectares impacting 4 million farm families. An additional 2 million farm families may have yield increases by 1 ton/ha on 2.5 million hectares. These gains would translate into 5 million tons of additional grain annually, adding $1.5 billion in value to smallholder incomes and lowering input (water, energy, fertilizer) costs at the same time. An additional 6 million low-income, livestock dependent households could see income gains of $350/year due to greater fodder availability. Indirectly, hundreds of millions of low-income consumers will benefit from greater access to staples as well as nutrient-dense legumes, dairy and poultry products.

- *African maize-based systems*: Sustainable intensification of production systems in Africa is currently being implemented, and substantial opportunities exist for integrating and building on global, regional and bilateral research and development efforts. Significant impacts are anticipated with 4 million beneficiaries expected to emerge from poverty with investments in maize-based systems alone across Africa. The goal of investments in drought tolerant maize, a single technology that would be combined with others, are to reach a total of about 30-40 million people in maize-based systems (La Rovere et al. 2010). Benefits of over $900 million would be distributed almost equally among producers and consumers and include both risk reduction and increases in income (La Rovere et al. 2010). Strategic nutrient management can avoid major environmental pollution problems from agricultural intensification.

- *Other regions*: Global research investments, as well as those in relevant production systems, can provide a basis for technology spillovers and substantial gains in many countries. USAID Missions in different regions will be able to integrate globally relevant component technologies and systems intensification models in partnership with CGIAR, U.S. universities, USDA and other partners. For example:

  - Lowland Central Africa: research in cassava, maize, banana and grain legumes will offer excellent opportunities for system-level gains and support of national level investments.

  - Southeast Asia: Progress in rice, maize, grain legumes and sweet potato, along with conservation agriculture practices to enhance resource-use efficiency will provide a solid basis for investment by USAID Missions and other bilateral or regional partners.

  - Middle East and Central Asia: Rust-resistant wheat, higher-yielding, disease- and drought-tolerant grain legumes and conservation agricultural practices will increase productivity and resilience.

  - Central America: Improved, acid-soil tolerant maize, disease- and drought-tolerant beans, disease-resistant banana and potato will be linked to value chain and market-access investments, providing both food security and system resilience that enables market-led diversification.

III. Enhancing Nutrition and Food Safety Through Agriculture

This theme recognizes the importance of ensuring that agricultural systems contribute to nutrition and health goals. This theme brings special emphasis to the multiple pathways by which agricultural research can be harnessed to improve nutrition. It will primarily focus on opportunities to improve availability and access to a high quality diet, particularly for women and young children. Through targeted research in the natural and social sciences, we will focus agricultural systems on improving nutrition through diversification of production systems, enhancing dietary diversity and nutrient density of foods and reducing postharvest losses. Research will integrate clinical, operational, agricultural, translational, and public health nutrition research for the diagnosis, prevention and treatment of malnutrition. This theme will support an integrated research program that focuses on translating knowledge and practice from research conducted into widespread development practice. This theme will also pay attention to food safety challenges with a focus on reducing contaminants in the food supply. This research theme will use a variety of tools in the natural and social sciences at the household level and all along the value chain and target research in key areas from breeding nutrient-dense crops to social science research to better understand the primary determinants of child undernutrition in key production systems.

While the research priorities in the first two themes were selected for their potential to improve nutrition through increased incomes, food availability, and sustainability of production systems, thereby providing greater stability in production year-to-year, this research theme will examine investment opportunities on research focused on greater accessibility to high quality foods, its utilization, and ultimately improved human health. This theme recognizes that improved nutritional status and human health are dependant not only on food availability and accessibility, but also upon an individual's ability to absorb and utilize nutrients which is inherently influenced by an individual's health status and environmental factors. Therefore, the implementation of relevant research programs under this theme will be, to the extent possible, coordinated with country-level operations research and programs under both FTF and other programs under the Global Health Initiative and Secretary Clinton's 1,000-Days Campaign to improve maternal and child health.

Several important objectives related to improving dietary quality, food safety and nutrition include:

- Increasing the availability of, access to, and consumption of nutrient-dense foods, such as animal source foods and legumes, by women and children, and increasing the nutrient content of key staples through biofortification;

- Developing new means for reducing and preventing agricultural and food safety threats, notably zoonotic diseases and mycotoxin contamination; and

- Designing sustainable intensification technology, management practices and policy research to ensure that water and other system factors promote nutrition and health and complement interventions that underpin food security for marginal and vulnerable communities.

Within the poverty and hunger reduction context of the *Feed the Future* initiative, the following are examples of important research priorities that emerge from the constraints and opportunity analysis:

Grain Legume Productivity Gains

Globally, grain legumes are grown on almost 200 million hectares, primarily in developing countries (CIAT et al. 2010). Demand for grain legumes is expected to grow by 1 percent per year through 2020 (CIAT et al. 2010). At the same time, much greater productivity gains in cereals during the past 40 years has contributed to displacement of bean, cowpea, lentil, chickpea, pigeonpea and other legume foods in farming systems reducing the supply of affordable legumes and contributing to negative nutritional outcomes (such as a higher prevalence of iron-deficiency anemia in South Asia) (CIAT et al. 2010). The optimal ratio of cereal to legume foods in traditional diets is 2 to1, but due to low yields and higher prices, that ratio in South and Southeast Asia has now reached 9 to 1 (CIAT et al. 2010). Grain legumes are also vital components of sustainably intensifying systems, improving soil fertility and raising the yields of subsequent crops by increasing soil nitrogen. Finally, legumes drive smallholder incomes in both local and regional markets, and represent an important means of reducing poverty. Key research opportunities in these crops include:

- *Expand climbing bean range in Africa:* Improvement and adoption of climbing beans in the East African highlands is leading to major yield increases, with more than 3 tons/ha being readily reached. The scope for increasing both the penetration and productivity of this technology is excellent, making it a key component of sustainable intensification in the region.

- *Enhanced targeting of improved rhizobia:* Rhizobium species of bacteria are key to increasing biological nitrogen fixation. Research can identify key alignments of these critical organisms along with specific traits in important leguminous crops. Grain legume crops will also be improved so as to enhance the efficiency of nitrogen fixation in the plant.

- *Target key pests and diseases of legumes in select systems:* Research that overcomes key constraints can have transformative impacts on grain legume crop production. Overcoming pests and diseases has raised yields of chickpea in cool season areas yet more work is needed. In South Asia, lentil and mungbean yields can be improved as part of a diversified, sustainably intensified South Asian system, which will have impacts on productivity of other crops in the system. In West Africa, ongoing research on Bt cowpea holds great potential to reduce pest losses to this important legume.

Increase Micronutrient Density and Bioavailability

Biofortification has emerged as a highly strategic opportunity for addressing micronutrient deficiency, also known as "hidden hunger." While not a silver bullet, biofortified crops can complement fortification and supplementation strategies, and may be especially effective in reaching those communities where other interventions are particularly expensive or difficult. Further, integration of biofortified crops into production systems will consider the role of these foods in the context of the whole diet, to ensure attention to bioavailability of critical nutrients. Key opportunities include:

- *High-zinc, high-iron and high-Vitamin A rice:* Though high-zinc rice has been achieved, increasing iron content to levels sufficient to prevent and control anemia will likely require transgenic approaches utilizing iron-rich proteins from grain legumes. Ongoing research is also developing beta-carotene (pro-Vitamin A) rich rice. These examples illustrate feasibility but require additional research and development.

- *Vitamin A-rich sweet potato, iron-enhanced beans and other crops:* Key opportunities exist to address micronutrient deficiencies in Africa and some of the poorest regions of Asia and Latin America. Iron-enriched beans are currently being adopted in part of the East Africa highlands, and the scope for integrating the trait into higher-yielding climbing varieties is excellent. In hotter and drier areas, orange-fleshed sweet potatoes have been shown to raise serum retinol (Vitamin A) among schoolchildren, representing an important and sustainable means of combating widespread deficiency among low-income families.

Reduce/Eliminate Mycotoxin Contamination of Staple Crops

Under tropical conditions, fungi can attack pre- and post-harvest and cause dangerous build-ups of mycotoxins such as aflatoxin. These are powerful anti-nutrients, undermining the immune system and overall health and nutrition. Potential investment areas under FTF include:

- *Aflatoxin resistance*: While many non-research interventions will be useful, upstream research alliances could potentially develop new traits that directly combat infection by the fungus, while downstream research efforts can examine opportunities for biocontrol making this an exciting area for developing new approaches to address this issue in the near and long term. Potential priority crops include maize and groundnut.

Reduce Post-Harvest Losses

A range of pests and diseases attack crops pre- and post-harvest, accounting for billions of dollars of losses every year. In other cases, non-research interventions are needed (such as improved storage and transport conditions), but in some cases research can provide new means for preventing pest infestation and losses that affect incomes and food security. Integrated pest management can help protect value and quality both in the field, from the field to the market, all the way to the end user.

- *Protecting vegetables from pest damage*: Some globally important vegetable crops (cabbage, tomato, etc.) will benefit from research to develop better bio-control of pests that damage the product both before and after harvest.

PART THREE. CROSS-CUTTING ISSUES

Cross-cutting issues that span global technology development, regional adaptation and local systems intensification will be integrated at all levels in implementing the research strategy. Three key cross-cutting issues, identified under FTF, will be emphasized: gender, climate change and the environment.

Gender

As has been emphasized throughout this strategy document, gender cannot just be addressed as an add-on but, rather, must be integrated throughout the research planning and execution process. This will be a new way of doing business for many and thus resources and training will need to be deployed towards efforts to assess when the constraints to production to women and men producers are the same, and when they are different. When they are different, for example, when certain crops are largely grown by women or when women are the main marketers of certain products, we will ensure that our research is addressing the constraints faced by women in producing and marketing these crops. Toward this end we will:

- ensure that women as well as men are active participants in the process of research planning and research management, receiving the training and skills they need,
- evaluate impacts of all research on both women and men and adjust our programs to ensure that both benefit,
- measure our progress through changes in incomes of both women and men in rural areas,
- ensure that women, as agricultural producers, have access to assets, inputs and technologies,
- ensure that the technologies we develop respond to women's needs and roles,
- fund new research to develop and share best practices for integrating gender research
- advance women's leadership in science and technology through proactive recruitment, mentoring, and targeted research support.

Climate Change

Climate change, though difficult to predict with any precision, needs to be addressed as a cornerstone of the FTF initiative. The World Bank's *World Development Report* for 2008 noted that climate change impacts on agriculture will disproportionately affect the poor who depend on agriculture for livelihoods and who have a lower capacity to adapt. Challenges associated with changing climatic conditions and increased climatic and weather variability are being factored into R&D planning at every level, from cutting-edge research on photosynthetic efficiency all the way through to land and water management on farm. Research has a key role in generating technologies, management practices and policies that help developing country farmers, herders, fishers and forest-dwellers adapt to a changing climate. Productivity growth and resilience can and must advance hand-in-hand.

Agriculture is both a driver of climate change, as well as one of the most vulnerable sectors. However it also has important climate change mitigation and adaptation potential. Globally, it is estimated that agriculture accounts for 15 percent of greenhouse gas (GHG) emissions with an additional 18 percent of global GHG emissions resulting from land use changes and forestry (WRI

2005). For GHG emissions associated with land use changes, tropical deforestation for conversion to agricultural land is the largest source. This underscores the surprising fact that 80 percent of agricultural emissions are generated in developing countries. The global role underscores both the needs and opportunities from seeing agriculture as part of a highly inter-linked global debate and response.

Box 4. Climate Change: New Insights on Adaptation and Mitigation

Climate change models show that the developing world, including some of the most food insecure areas, will face rapid and largely negative impacts. With agriculture being a main source of employment, climate change threatens both food production and the most important source of income for the poor. Fortunately, science is opening channels for tackling some of the most challenging problems facing farmers—drought, heat, salinity and new pests and diseases. The United States is uniquely positioned to work with countries around the world in facing these threats.

New research shows that agricultural intensification has actually reduced greenhouse gas emissions compared to what would have been generated using traditional production practices. Despite increased emission levels associated with fertilizer use, up to 161 gigatons of Carbon were not released during the last 50 years due to sustainable intensification of agricultural production (Burney et al. 2010). For each dollar invested in agricultural productivity, an estimated 68kg less carbon has been released (Burney et al. 2010). This compares favorably with other proposed mitigation strategies.

The following considerations will guide our research investments—and in fact are reflected in our earlier discussion of the FTF research themes and the likely areas of investment:

- Adaptation to greater climatic variability as well as longer-term climate shifts means intensifying stress tolerance while at the same time judiciously exploring and deploying genetic diversity of crop plants and livestock. Thus traits such as abiotic stress tolerance (such as drought, heat and other environmental stress) to crop and livestock disease ranges and severity (such as potato late blight and rift valley fever).

- Advances in modeling of climates, production systems and actual or potential threats (e.g. pathogens, drought) can help guide research investments.

- New technologies for resource use efficiency can reduce costs while also reducing greenhouse gas emissions. Here key technologies around nitrogen-use efficiency and pest resistance can increase productivity and incomes, have positive environmental impacts, and at the same time reduce emissions.

- A number of interventions related to soil fertility and land management will have both mitigation and adaptation benefits. For example, integration of leguminous trees in agroforestry systems can both increase fertility and crop yields, as well as contribute to higher levels of carbon sequestration in soils, with accompanying increases in water-holding capacity.

Environment

The FTF research strategy recognizes the interconnections of ecosystems services to agriculture and the health and well-being of local communities. Thus, across all three research themes, there is a need to map the potential environmental impacts across a range of indicators, and to demonstrate a clear understanding of how the proposed technologies or approaches impact the local environment. FTF recognizes the importance of increased agricultural productivity to reduce the transition of new lands to active agriculture production, thereby conserving natural areas which can even contribute directly as a food source for many local communities. The FTF research portfolio will integrate attention to the technologies, policies and management practices that foster natural resource conservation and the integration of productive agriculture in the larger landscape. Both direct and indirect environmental benefits will be considered. The following are illustrative examples of the recognition within FTF of the importance of environmental considerations in the drive to sustainably increase agricultural productivity.

- Sustainable intensification of production systems can help reduce pressures driving agricultural conversion of watersheds, rangeland, wetlands and forests.

- At the systems level, conservation agriculture practices will increase water and nutrient use efficiency and further strengthen resilience of the production system. Shifts towards applying reduced and no-till systems can mean greater water penetration and moisture retention in soils, which will have significant impacts on the local environment and the ecosystem services it provides.

- Climate change adaptation approaches, in addition to enhancing communities' resiliency, can have significant positive ecological impacts, such as encouraging the re-infiltration of groundwater and the rehabilitation of other natural storage systems.

- The development of more sustainable aquaculture and fisheries management technologies and approaches can have indirect positive impacts on coastal ecosystems.

- Research to increase livestock productivity can lead to improvements in household economic security, and can concomitantly pursue strategies that reduce adverse environmental impacts such as GHG emissions.

PART FOUR. ACCOUNTABILITY AND IMPACT

Expected impacts of research investments fit squarely within the FTF Results Framework, with research on agricultural technologies, natural resource management practices, and policy contributing to improved agricultural productivity and thus agricultural sector growth, which in turn contributes to reductions in hunger and poverty. The research programs funded will report against the FTF indicators, which include the number of new technologies developed and adopted by farmers (both women and men and by income level) as well as ultimate impacts on changes in the levels of income and measures of nutritional status. Impact assessments of past agricultural investments have been commissioned, to better understand the links between technology development and adoption and ultimate impacts on poverty and hunger. Research to improve priority assessments of research areas and impact evaluation are integral elements of this strategy and will ensure that we integrate new information when allocating resources.

Through close collaboration with partners (farmer organizations, NGOs, and researchers in developing countries and the international agriculture research centers), critical feedback on the potential for impact, likelihood of adoption, and other factors which are integrated into ex ante impact assessments will be collected and assessed. These analyses will assist in developing criteria to select research projects with the greatest potential impact. It will be an iterative process, whereby new information, as appropriate, is integrated into our project review.

Monitoring and evaluation of research projects will be core elements of the research strategy to ensure accountability. We will integrate evaluation into all phases of the research programs. Through close collaboration with the research community and other stakeholders, we will identify important measures that capture both the quality of research and the relevance of the outcomes it produces. We will work with the research community to identify topic-specific criteria for evaluation to ensure relevance for each program. Monitoring and evaluation will require countries to regularly collect data and strengthen their data development capacity. We will coordinate our data development activity with those undertaken by other partners, including the major UN-headed Global Strategy to Improve Agricultural and Rural Statistics.

Different approaches for monitoring and evaluation will be used with different partners, though our standards remain the same, including monitoring and evaluation of the gender impacts of our investments by establishing with our partners gender-disaggregated targets, tracking these impacts of our investments on women and men, and measuring the progress of women's achievements relative to men's. With CGIAR partners, we are actively engaged in crafting the systems for monitoring progress evaluation and impact assessment of their research activities. The new CGIAR reform process will ensure greater accountability and we will work closely with the established mechanisms to ensure our resources are well spent and that targeted milestones are being accomplished.

Similarly, research investments projects at US universities and other similar research institutions will be closely monitored. Program officers will assess performance and ensure timely achievements of milestones. Where FTF resources are leveraging those of private sector partners, we will ensure up-front that priorities and goals are aligned to help ensure that funds are well spent and that all partners are equally invested in timely performance. But the monitoring process does not stop there, as program officers will work closely with appropriate partners in private sector collaborations to ensure continued progress towards goals through routine reporting and oversight.

Following well-developed best-practices, proposals submitted for funding will identify up-front the ways that progress can be evaluated and demonstrate that the proposed approach is likely to have a significant impact. Where higher risk ideas are proposed, broader impacts will be expected Subsequent collaborative engagement between program officers and grant awardees will ensure that milestones are identified, timetables are developed, and updates on progress will be communicated through routine reporting that will be shared with research partners, such as those in the national programs as appropriate.

In each case, program officers will work closely with researchers to implement course corrections where necessary, or even terminate projects.

The key to broad impact is ensuring that the necessary linkages between research and systems for deployment are developed, strengthened and/or supported. Global research investments will be linked with national research activities supported through local Missions and other development partners to ensure relevance at the farm or community level. Further, we will support research to better understand deployment pathways to increase impact at the farm and community levels.

PART FIVE.
IMPLEMENTING THE STRATEGY - CHANGING HOW WE WORK

Achieving this vision of increased agricultural productivity to decrease poverty and hunger will require a restructuring of agricultural research systems globally by forging greater linkages among global and local/regional research organizations and donors (such as USAID, universities, national programs in developing countries, CGIAR, USDA and other government research institutes, and the private sector). We will also include knowledge sharing at the country level to ensure the relevance of global research at the farm level and greater efficiency in our efforts to transfer technologies and innovations for local adaptation. Fostering pathways for deployment of innovations from laboratory to farm will require strengthening the linkages between upstream fundamental research and downstream (more applied) research partners.

All the partners—funders, researchers, and implementers—whether in developed or developing countries will need to commit to stronger, results-driven partnerships. U.S. commitment to this new vision and strategy is being demonstrated through a commitment to substantial increase in resources for global research and development compared to recent years. While FTF focus countries are key targets of this strategy, coordination and collaborations with strategic partner countries and our support to regional and sub-regional research organizations will ensure broad spillovers to other food-insecure countries.

Improved coordination among the range of research partners will enable each institution to contribute to the goals of reducing poverty and hunger by focusing on its comparative advantage in addressing the challenges of food insecurity. Each will be recognized for their critical role in the complex process of reducing food insecurity and alleviating poverty by contributing along the continuum of research, development and deployment, from upstream, basic science to downstream applications at the community level. We will leverage the capacities of different partners such as university researchers' theoretical contributions in the natural and social sciences, private sector's expertise in basic research and in effectively deploying technology and innovations, and partners in national agricultural research programs in developing countries who have deep knowledge of local farmer needs. These comparative strengths will be brought together to ensure appropriate technologies and innovations reach the hands of farmers to improve food security and child nutrition and increase farmer incomes.

Leadership in the global development community

The U.S. is unique in the world in being able to marshal the world's largest agricultural research and teaching community—public and private—as partners in a global struggle to achieve lasting food security. Feed the Future provides a blueprint for working with partners around the world to achieve a strong focus on productivity gains, sound policy, and sustainable management of natural resources and the environment. The USG will promote FTF goals and strategies both in their own research investments and through their international partnerships. For example, working closely with other development agencies, USAID will ensure that its country, regional, and global investments reflect the FTF Research Strategy, and fully align for greatest impact. This will include working through its key regional fora in Africa, Asia and Latin America to ensure that country-led strategies prioritize research, related capacity building and other key investments supporting sustainable agriculture intensification (seed and fertilizer markets, output markets, extension, and others). The Department of State, USDA, the Department of the Treasury and other agencies will also promote strategic alignment in important fora, such as the United Nations Food and Agriculture Organization (FAO), the International Fund for Agricultural Development (IFAD) and others.

Capacity Building

A separate capacity building strategy will provide the details regarding how the overall alignment of objectives and investments will occur. The following capacity building principles will be taken into consideration while implementing the FTF research strategy and designing the capacity building strategy:

- strengthen capacity of developing country farmers and rural households to take advantage of new scientific innovations and technologies
- develop capacity at the individual, organizational, and network levels
- integrate capacity development and research investments to maximize impact
- consider capacity needs for monitoring and evaluation (M&E)

Whole of Government

USAID and USDA will collaborate to strengthen the synergies among U.S. agricultural research groups (U.S. universities, USDA, private sector), CGIAR centers and national research programs in developing countries to engage in research that will advance global food security goals, focusing the comparative advantages of each group on addressing specific constraints. USAID and USDA will also coordinate to reach out to the National Science Foundation and the National Institutes of Health and other USG agencies to identify research areas where common interest and opportunity exists to achieve FTF goals. This will leverage much larger public and private investments in U.S. research capacity to target science that supports the global effort but will also benefit U.S. agriculture, especially in the area of promoting productivity growth through science-based innovation. USDA will review its on-going and planned research programs to identify areas for "dual-use" benefits with relevance to both FTF and U.S. agriculture.

USDA-USAID Partnerships

One important strategy for enhancing food security outcomes from USG investments will be the Norman Borlaug Commemorative Research Initiative. USDA and USAID will work together to identify opportunities for leveraging USDA research investments to advance FTF research and development goals through the Norman Borlaug Commemorative Research Initiative. The partnership between USAID and USDA is based on the principle that international public goods-type knowledge can lead to increased agriculture productivity both in the United States and developing countries. Such 'dual use' includes research regarding adaptation of crops to better cope with climate change, production of livestock vaccines to recalcitrant infectious diseases, and efficiency in water and energy use in agriculture. All such knowledge will be widely applicable even though regional adaptation of principles will be necessary.

USDA-Direct: USAID Support to Intra-mural programs: Towards this endeavor, we will work together to identify USDA intramural programs and existing USAID funded research programs for which additional monetary resources would result in major benefits to the global food security agenda. We will seek to determine where a comparative advantage exists for solving specific problems through utilizing the capabilities of advanced labs in the United States that are not available in the developing countries. USAID and USDA will work together to identify and manage research investments where partnerships and resources linked to FTF objectives would help generate dual-purpose high-impact outcomes (benefits U.S. and developing world agriculture) and significant impacts from the research. USAID and USDA have a long history of collaboration. Expanded efforts that support stronger engagement by leveraging USDA research with development partners are planned in areas such as:

- Wheat stem rust—via close linkages with CGIAR and U.S. university partners
- Livestock Diseases: East Coast and Rift Valley Fevers with CGIAR
- White fly resistance—IPM for virus disease vector control
- Genetic Resources—strengthen cooperation between the National Plant Germplasm System, CGIAR and the Global Crop Diversity Trust
- Marker-assisted technologies in key crop diseases
- Food safety, especially reducing mycotoxins in crops
- Increasing legume productivity

National Institute of Food and Agriculture—USDA/NIFA-USAID complementary programming: A new aspect of whole of government cooperation under the FTF will be complementary funding from USDA to deepen and increase the relevance of NIFA research partnerships to FTF goals. Close cooperation between USAID and USDA will enable new global partnerships that link frontier research in the United States with partners in the developing world, increasing relevance of research to food security constraints and maximizing potential development impacts. Key opportunities emerging from the priorities include:

- Tolerance to drought, heat and other stresses
- Food safety and quality factors, including resistance to mycotoxin contamination
- USDA-university collaborations around major diseases and genetics of livestock
- A wide range of new approaches that align with priority constraints.

Refocused CGIAR Research

As indicated above, increased investments will directly engage global partnerships that span among regional partners, CGIAR and advanced research institutions in the U.S. and elsewhere. Moreover, CGIAR programs that are integrating large-scale core breeding capabilities in staple crops as well as applying multi-disciplinary approaches to production systems intensification will provide critical linkages to broad sets of partners at the regional and national levels. We will emphasize key flagship technologies and outputs as well as the integrative, on-the-ground capacities of emerging so-called CGIAR research-programs.

The CGIAR system's restructuring is already underway. Continued U.S. leadership in this effort is focused on a more output- and impact-oriented structuring of CGIAR global research programs. USAID will continue working very closely with the World Bank, DFID, the Bill and Melinda Gates Foundation, the European Community, CIDA-Canada, and Australia (AUSAID and ACIAR) and other partners on three areas:

- *Governance structure:* a new model for CGIAR governance spanning all the centers in the CGIAR Consortium has been put in place.

- *Alignment of funding:* establishment of a new CGIAR Fund at the World Bank to achieve tighter strategic focus and direction to donor engagement and support of the system is was completed in 2010 and is entering its initial year of implementation in 2011.

- *Development of new CGIAR research programs:* these thematic programs span individual CGIAR centers to unite them regarding goals, resources and approach to global problems pertaining to agriculture including policy and environmental issues.

The CGIAR's expanded emphasis on impacts and deliverables through multi-center-led programs, as well as partnerships with both upstream and downstream research programs, makes this an ideal time to link to FTF research programs.

USAID Competitive Grant Programs

USAID provides an array of competitive opportunities which span various research partners. The major partnership with the Land Grant university community is the Collaborative Research Support Programs (CRSPs), which offers an important means of supporting and shaping that community's involvement in research for development and food security. CRSP programs by definition emphasize human resource capacity development and developing country partnerships, and as a community they are strategically positioned to take a leading role, along with the broader university research community. Other competitive programs, for example in biotechnology, feature university-led and public-private partnerships that carry out research and build capacity. Feed the Future offers the opportunity to expand CRSP cooperation with USDA programs, as well as provides the potential for linking both with CGIAR research programs. In addition:

- New grants will be strategically targeted on solving key constraints at scale. This means a focus on fewer and larger research activities to increase the scale of impact.

- We will seek to include the development/extension/application components of research and development in the grants, emphasizing impact pathways in addition to basic research. This will foster expanded partnerships across universities, USDA, CGIAR, private sector, and local partners, as well as more direct engagement of USAID field missions.

- There will be enhanced opportunities to more closely link to investments in the CGIAR in ways that expand impact, or to address constraints where the CGIAR does not have predominant capability.

USG, Private Sector, and Industry-linked Partnerships

Partnerships with U.S. and international private sector will play a key role in this strategy. Engaging the private sector-led Global Harvest Initiative provides opportunities to leverage private sector strengths in the areas that are important to agriculture in developing countries such as historical analysis of agricultural productivity and in industry experience with development and deployment of new technologies. In strategic investments in biotechnology, in particular, sophisticated product development expertise is needed. Many of the genetic/production traits being addressed by industry are readily applicable in developing country crops and settings, making them strategic partners to researchers in developing countries. Private sector partnerships can also provide access to important traits around drought and heat resistance, nutrient use efficiency and other areas where the U.S. private sector is investing heavily. These collaborative programs provide important lessons for both upstream (basic research) and downstream (applied and implementation research) partnerships in developing countries, and will emphasize research timelines and clear product development strategies that can be useful models for other research under the initiative.

CONCLUSION

The Millennium Development Goal of reducing hunger and poverty is ambitious an objective, but it can be achieved with strategic investment in agriculture and rural development. The US Government response to this challenge is the FTF Initiative which has adopted the goals to address the root causes of hunger and to establish a lasting foundation for change by aligning our resources with country-owned processes through sustained, multi-stakeholder partnerships. The research strategy presented here illustrates how USG resources will be targeted to examine and address root causes of hunger through expanding the productivity of key staple crops, transforming production systems where poverty and hunger are prevalent, and improving the quality and safety of the diet of rural farm families. These research endeavors are tightly linked to the concerted effort in building, both in the United States and our developing country partners, a lasting foundation of human and institutional capacity to address the growing challenges to agriculture in the 21st Century.

The path will not be easy, nor can we know all the challenges that we will encounter, but the stakes are high and the commitment is real. We cannot act alone. An explicit objective of this strategy is its intentional leveraging of resources from many partners – including our developing country partners, donors, the CGIAR, academia, the NGO community, and private sector partners. As each partner contributes, so too will the recognition be shared among the many actors necessary to bring agricultural research innovations from the laboratory to the farm. Though circumstances will change and new information will emerge, the strength of FTF is that it will lay down an institutional foundation to advance a strategic and relevant research agenda in addressing global food security.

Our intention is to encourage strategic alignment of research investments with FTF goals, recognizing that specific situations will require taking a variety of factors into account. With additional information on country priorities, resource levels and existing program objectives, strategic planning can be undertaken for a given new program. In addition, although the research strategy has been developed to guide research investments associated with FTF, an on-going and robust dialogue with partners across the U.S. and international research communities will both foster broader relevance of the strategy and help marshall other resources in support of FTF goals. Through close coordination with our developing country partners, a refocused research agenda will also shape partnerships with other donors and the international and US-based research communities.

Research figures prominently in FTF because it is critical to enhancing and sustaining agricultural productivity growth and improving nutrition, which are strongly linked to economic growth in developing countries and reduced poverty—both essential elements of sustainable food security. Though the goals are ambitious, the magnitude of food insecurity world-wide demands coordinated and focused efforts to improve agricultural productivity for smallholder farm families in the developing world. Success will be measured in agricultural systems that more effectively and efficiently harness fundamental biological and physical processes in ways that meet the needs of the poor and the hungry. At the same time, these transformations must conserve the resource base in both highly productive and less productive areas. The transformations required to achieve these goals will only be possible if the Initiative is underpinned by innovative research and partnerships, strategically directed towards achieving the Millennium Development Goal of reducing poverty and hunger.

BIBLIOGRAPHY

Alston, Julian, Connie Chang-Kang, Michele C. Marra, Philip G. Pardey and TJ Wyatt. 2000. *A Meta-Analysis of Rates of Return to Agricultural R&D*. Research Report 113, International Food Policy Research Institute, Washington, DC.

African Union - Inter-African Bureau for Animal Resources (AU-IBAR). 2010. Focus area fact sheets. Accessed Dec 23, 2010. http://www.au-ibar.org/index.php/en/focus-areas/trypanosomiasis

Baumert, K., T. Herzog, and J. Pershing. 2005. Navigating the Numbers: Greenhouse Gas Data and International Climate Policy. World Resources Institute.

Bruinsma, J. 2009. The resource outlook to 2050: By how much do land, water and crop yields need to increase by 2050? Expert Meeting on How to Feed the World in 2050. FAO. Rome.

Burney, J., S.J. Davis, and D.B. Lobell. 2010. Greenhouse gas mitigation by agricultural intensification. *Proceedings of the National Academy of Sciences*. 107(26): 12052-12057.

CIP. 2010. Potato / Late Blight Late blight Overview. http://www.cipotato.org/potato/pests_diseases/late_blight/ Accessed 12/29/10.

Coulibaly, O., C. Aitchedji, S. Gbegbelegbe, H. Mignouna and J. Lowenberg-DeBoer. 2008. Baseline Study for Impact Assessment of High Quality Insect Resistant Cowpea in West Africa. Nairobi, Kenya: African Agricultural Technology Foundation

Dalrymple, D. 2008. "International agricultural research as a global public good: concepts, the CGIAR experience and policy issues," Journal of International Development, John Wiley & Sons, Ltd., vol. 20(3), pages 347-379.

Di Giulio G, G. Lynen, S. Morzaria, C. Oura, R. Bishop. 2009. Live immunization against East Coast fever--current status. Trends Parasitol. 25(2):85-92. Epub 2009 Jan 8.

Evenson, R. and Rosegrant, M. (2003). "The economic consequences of crop genetic improvement programmes" In: Evenson, R'.E., Gollin, D. (Eds.), Crop Genetic Improvement and Agricultural Developmenat. CABI.

FAOSTAT. Food and Agriculture Organization. http://faostat.fao.org/default.aspx Accessed Dec 2010.

FAO. 2008. Wheat Rust Disease Global Program. Crisis Management Centre for the Food Chain/Plant Protection. Food and Agriculture Organization of the UN. Rome. Available at: http://www.fao.org/agriculture/crops/core-themes/theme/pests/wrdgp/en/

GRiSP. 2010. Sustainable crop productivity increase for global food security: A CGIAR Research Program on Rice-Based Production Systems. November 2010, IRRI, AfricaRice, CIAT.

World Bank. 2007. From Agriculture to Nutrition: Pathways, Synergies and Outcomes. Agriculture and Rural Development Department. The International Bank for Reconstruction and Development. Washington, D.C.

IFPRI. 2009. Annual Report 2009. The Power of Many. Available at: http://irri.org/about-irri/annual-reports/annual-report-2009/the-power-of-many. Accessed 12/29/10.

IRRI. 2010a. Submergence Tolerance. http://beta.irri.org/projects15/en/stresses/submergence-tolerance. Accessed 12/29/10.

IRRI. 2010b. Drought-Tolerant Rice. http://beta.irri.org/projects15/en/stresses/drought-tolerant-rice. Accessed 12/29/10.

La Rovere, R., G. Kostandini, T. Abdoulaye, J. Dixon, W. Mwangi, Z. Guo, and M. Bänziger. 2010. Potential impact of investments in drought tolerant maize in Africa. CIMMYT, Addis Ababa, Ethiopia.

Ortiz, R., K. Sayre, B. Govaerts, R. Gupta, G.V. Subbarao, T. Ban, D. Hodson, J. M. Dixon, J. I. Ortiz-Monasterio, M. Reynolds. 2008. Climate change: Can wheat beat the heat? Agriculture, Ecosystems & Environment. 126:46-58.

Royal Society. 2009. Reaping the Benefits: Science and the sustainable intensification of global agriculture. RS Policy Document 11/09. London. p. 25-26.

Shapouri, S., M. Peters, S. Allen, S. Rosen, F. Baquedano. 2010. Food Security Assessment, 2010-20. US Dept. of Agriculture/Economic Research Service. GFA-21.

Spielman D.J. 2008. *In*: National Academies of Science, Washington, Public-Private Partnerships and Pro-Poor Livestock Research: p. 263 The Search for an East Coast Fever Vaccine

Thirtle, Colin, Lin Lin and Jenifer Piesse. 2003. The impact of research-led agricultural productivity growth on poverty reduction in Africa, Asia and Latin America. *World Development* 31, 12: 1959-1975.

Thomson, G.R. 2005. Contagious bovine pleuropneumonia and poverty: A strategy for addressing the effects of the disease in sub-Saharan Africa. Research report, DFID Animal Health Programme, Centre for Tropical Veterinary Medicine, University of Edinburgh, UK.

Timmer, P. 2005. Agriculture and Pro-Poor Growth: An Asian Perspective. Center for Global Development. Working Paper 63.

Tran, D. 2004. Hybrid Rice for Food Security. Fact Sheet. FAO. www.fao.org/rice2004/en/f-sheet/factsheet6.pdf Accessed 12/29/10.

World Development Report 2008: Agriculture for Development. 2007. The World Bank. Washington, DC.

WHO. 2010. Rift Valley Fever Fact Sheet. http://www.who.int/mediacentre/factsheets/fs207/en/ Accessed 12/29/2010.

www.ingramcontent.com/pod-product-compliance
Lightning Source LLC
Chambersburg PA
CBHW080614180526
45168CB00007B/2914